THE IRISH UPRISING

HOW KEANO AND THE MIGHTY QUINN SAVED SUNDERLAND

ANDY DAWSON

SPORTS
BOOKS

Published in Great Britain by
SportsBooks Limited
PO Box 422
Cheltenham
GL50 2YN

Tel: +44 (0) 1242 256755
email: info@sportsbooks.ltd.uk
www.sportsbooks.ltd.uk

Cover design by Alan Hunns
Photographs by Craig Leng

A catalogue record for this book is available from
the British Library.

ISBN 9781899807 60 4

Printed in England by Mackays of Chatham, plc

To Dionne and Mia Lucy – for your love, support and patience throughout both the writing of this book and my ongoing and inexplicable obsession with Sunderland AFC.

CONTENTS

FOREWORD

BY CHARLIE HURLEY

I SUPPOSE AT the start of last season when we were at the bottom and Roy Keane took over, the best we could have hoped for would have been to make the play-offs. But here we are back where we belong, in the Premiership and as champions. Who would have believed that was possible?

But you see Roy's a Cork man – as I am – and Niall Quinn's from Dublin, so everything is possible. We've got that attitude in Ireland that we will not be beaten.

You can feel the buzz is back in Sunderland and you know that Roy really believes it when he says he's not frightened of Manchester United or Chelsea. Champions next season? Don't bet against it.

Seriously, if we are in the top half in our first season back we'll have done well. But you just never know with Roy in charge. He's a winner. He was a bit of a dirty player now and then but he was a great player and a great leader.

I think what he brings to management is control. He's very calm. If you are having problems in a game you look across and instead of someone jumping about like a banshee there he is, standing there very controlled. And as a player that gives you confidence.

Niall has recognised no club is any good without its fans and he has set about trying to get those who'd decided they'd had enough back to the Stadium of Light. The Sunderland fans are the best in the country but you could understand why some had decided they wouldn't renew their season tickets.

They'd not had a lot to shout about over the last few years with success followed by lack of investment and inevitable failure. But Niall and the Irish consortium have backed their words with deeds. Their attitude is very positive and I believe the stadium will be full to bursting this season. I'm sure of that.

INTRODUCTION

AS I'M WRITING this, Sunderland, the football club allotted to me at birth, have just announced that they've broken the British transfer record for a goalkeeper, paying £9 million for Craig Gordon of Hearts. During my lifetime of following the team, we haven't broken too many records, especially not positive ones.

Most recently we captured the record for the lowest points total in a Premiership season (19 in 2003) and then smashed it with our next attempt (15 in 2006). But it's said that a good goalkeeper will win a team 15 points over the course of a season – does that mean we're already just a point away from being better than the class of 2006?

It's more than 25 years since I went to my first match and I've never felt more optimistic about the long-term future at Sunderland. Since that first game (7th March 1981, home against Aston Villa; we lost 2-1,) I thought I'd more or less been through it all, good and bad. For example, there were a few trips to Wembley, every single one ending in varying degrees of disappointment.

There were those few months in 1983 when Frank Worthington played for us, and the best part of the afternoon was getting there early enough to watch him warm up and do things that I'd never imagined a human being could do with a football. Days that included 26th February 1983, when my dad, an AA patrolman, got free tickets from Ally McCoist as a thank you for mending his car, then getting to meet Ally after the game but being so star struck that I was incapable of speech. Not to mention almost being crushed to death twice during the Milk Cup run of 1985 – once in the Fulwell End and once in the Roker.

There was the club's first and only relegation to the Third Division in 1987, when the pain of it all was too much to bear and I toyed with the idea of supporting Hull City for a while, for reasons which I still don't quite understand. My fury at missing just one home match in the 1990/91 season; locked out against Liverpool when I was three places away from the front of the queue only for the turnstile to close because the ground was full of part-timers who'd come to gawp at the league champions.

There was the pain and abject misery caused by Terry Butcher's managerial reign, and his swift and systematic destruction of the gradual progress that had been made in the previous few years – the idea that he was an acceptable choice to run the team seems just as wrong now as it did then. The arrival of Peter Reid and the jarring thought that 'Hmm, hang on a minute, he might just be pretty good for us.' Which he was, but then eventually, wasn't.

The football played under Reid for the first couple of years at the Stadium of Light was the best I've ever seen from players in the red and white. Then there was the goal-poacher extraordinaire that was Kevin Phillips, until he misguidedly decided he wanted to improve his 'all-round game' and started spending most of his time mooching about in midfield looking depressed.

Roy Keane blowing his top at the end of a 1-1 draw with Man U as he got himself sent off in the last minute, then Niall Quinn and Jason McAteer brilliantly and bravely taking the mickey out of him as he trudged off. The game against Charlton in 2003 when we scored three own goals against ourselves in the weirdest seven minutes of football I know I'll ever see, and then watching fans almost coming to blows with stewards who were refusing to let them leave the stadium before half-time.

The craziest incident of that gruesome 15 point season – 8th April 2006, against Fulham; walking over the Wearmouth Bridge towards the ground at 2.45pm, basking in the spring sunshine. By 3.21pm, the match had been abandoned due to a freak blizzard after Rory Delap had his nose broken when George McCartney slid into his face. That's right – a blizzard. In April.

Thinking things couldn't get any worse than when fans organised a 'white handkerchief' protest against the board, and my mate Noel took along one of his kid's (unused) disposable nappies to wave in the air as a display of his disgust. Thankfully realising that things really weren't going to get any worse when Niall Quinn's Drumaville consortium took control of the club and brought in Roy Keane as manager.

As I said the arrival of Quinn and Keane and their achievements during their first season together leaves me feeling more confident than I ever have been before about the future of the club that I've invested so much time, energy and disposable cash in for over a quarter of a century. As I write this and dream one of those silly, pointless football fan dreams about what might lie ahead, I feel as though I might finally be about to get some kind of real return on that investment.

With my tongue planted firmly in my cheek, I'd like to think that this book, the story of Drumaville's arrival and that dramatic season in the Championship, will be something we can all look back on, a reminder of where it all began, when Quinn and Keane are in their early '60's and celebrating Sunderland's tenth successive Champions League Final victory.

Silly, pointless football fan dreams. They're what keeps the game alive.

The Irish Uprising

CHAPTER ONE

IS ROY KEEN?

AS THE EXPRESSION on his face suddenly changed it was obvious that Richard Keys, Sky Sports' assured but disturbingly hairy-handed anchorman, had something very, very important to say. For now, all talk of the playful first-half mauling that Manchester United had just dealt out to a spineless Charlton Athletic side was to be momentarily forgotten. This was unrelated to the night's action – breaking news, something else from somewhere else, maybe a world-changing event. Famously, back in 1980, it was a sports presenter who told the American viewing public the shocking news of John Lennon's assassination, and now it looked as though Keys was on the brink of delivering a similarly earth-shattering thunderbolt. Had the Queen abdicated from the throne? Was the war on terror finally over? Perhaps Alan Shearer had choked to death on a cashew nut?

No, this was more, something in a different stratosphere. The viewing audience, consisting mostly of fans of Manchester United and Charlton Athletic plus those who had nothing better to do on a Wednesday evening in late August, closed their eyes with a mixture of fear and anticipation. And thus, Richard Keys did speak. And a smile spread across his thin lips as he revealed that, 'The new Sunderland manager is… it's Roy Keane.'

Eh? Keane? What the hell…?

In the subsequent hours the mobile phone network in and around Wearside practically buckled under the weight of thousands of text messages and garbled, gibbering phone calls as Sunderland fans spread the incredible news; incredible for two reasons. Firstly, the idea that a man as synonymous with success as Roy Keane was prepared to launch his managerial career with a club in such a state of punch-drunk upheaval as Sunderland was at the very least bizarre. It certainly proved that the man hadn't lost his lust for a good battle (or he had a hitherto unseen pitch-black sense of humour.) What was additionally incredible about the news was that it came less than 24 hours after Sunderland's temporary manager Niall Quinn had announced he'd sacked himself (which as club chairman he was perfectly entitled to do), and proclaimed that he would be bringing in a 'world class manager'.

At that point in time the term 'world class' applied to men like Fabio Capello or Frank Rijkaard – but it was now emerging that Sunderland's new world class manager would be someone who… well, someone who hadn't actually managed at any level. At all.

There was no doubting that Keane had been a world class player and a dominant personality at Manchester United where he spent 12 years hoovering up winner's medals, but managing at the very top of the game was very much not on his CV. Lifting trophies, excelling in the dispensing of on-field punishment, causing outrage in Irish society, those boxes had all been dutifully ticked, but not the one that boasted of world class managerial achievements.

But then it must be remembered that this is

Sunderland Association Football Club, a club with the most loyal of supporters and a huge, largely untapped amount of potential. Sadly, it's also a club which has an uncanny knack of cack-handedly snatching catastrophe from the jaws of success whenever possible, traumatising its fans and amusing the rest of the footballing world. This was the club who in the space of three years set the unwanted record of registering the lowest ever points total in the Premiership (a feeble, lily-livered 19) only to fecklessly smash that record at the very next attempt (an eye-watering and scarcely-believable 15). A club with a nearly-new stadium capable of holding almost fifty-thousand which had driven away most of its fan base through a series of unambitious and often downright clueless policy decisions. In fact, the only good thing about visiting the Stadium of Light by the spring of 2006 was that you didn't have to queue all that long for your half-time pint.

But a revolution took place on Wearside in the summer of 2006, and with it came the possibility that Sunderland's permanent role as one of football's eternal yo-yo clubs would soon be over. As the new club chairman and figurehead of the Drumaville consortium that had taken control of the club from the long-serving and widely disliked Bob Murray, former player Niall Quinn was hell-bent on restoring the trust that had evaporated between the fans and club and bringing some stability and an air of respectability back to the Black Cats.

In the early days of the takeover, Quinn compared his intentions to that of a wily card sharp, boasting, 'You don't play a game of poker by letting everybody know your hand, but my guys have a good hand'. It was probably best to ignore the fact that Quinn had quoted and broken the rule at the same, seemingly revealing to one and all the consortium's impressive financial muscle. Or maybe there was the possibility that, like a good poker player, he was just bluffing, but then that would mean that there was actually nothing in the Drumaville kitty.

Still, it looked as though the club was going to get a chairman who actually came out and communicated with the fans, unlike Quinn's predecessor. But the quality of the consortium's imaginary hand of cards was irrelevant – Quinn was brimming with enthusiasm and belief and it wouldn't take long for his fervour about what he described as 'a magic carpet ride' to spread across Wearside and beyond. Less gloriously he also said, 'This baby's been asleep for a few years now. But we want to wake her up and drive her forward', something which was just plain weird and made one wonder if he was eating too much cheese before bedtime.

Following the completion of the takeover by Quinn and his consortium of wealthy, self-made and mostly Irish businessmen, the club's chronic financial problems may have been on their way to being remedied, but a credible managerial appointment was absolutely vital if Sunderland weren't to continue oscillating between the divisions. Although Quinn had been unshaken in his determination from day one to bring to the club a manager who would be certain to take things forward, putting this idea into practice had proven to be much tougher.

Unwilling to carry on in the Sunderland tradition of settling for second best and patiently waiting for failure to inevitably come along, Quinn aimed high but found his plans swiftly scuppered when his two major targets both lost their nerve at the eleventh hour and decided not to join the club.

Ex-Celtic boss Martin O'Neill, who was choosing his moment before re-entering the managerial fray after a twelve-month sabbatical, took an age to deliberate before deciding not to come and help revitalise the club which he'd previously claimed to have supported as a boy. O'Neill would later pitch up at Aston Villa under the wing of Randy Lerner, the Midlands club's fascinatingly-named new billionaire owner, and would become embroiled in a skirmish with relegation from the Premiership.

The other name to be seriously linked with the job was Sam Allardyce, an ex-Sunderland player and a man who had taken Bolton Wanderers from nowhere, transforming them into a credible force with a cunning combination of shrewd purchasing, sports science, futuristic mobile phone headsets and direct, aggressive football.

At one point, Allardyce looked odds-on to drop down a division and later in the season, the Hull City manager Phil Brown (who had previously been Allardyce's right hand man at the Reebok Stadium) confirmed to the *Sunderland Echo* that his pal had been achingly close from walking away from Bolton for a crack at reviving Sunderland's fortunes. Brown would have linked up with his former boss on Wearside if Big Sam had made the move but it wasn't to be – Allardyce had one final season at Bolton, but appeared to be jaded and disinterested in it all, somehow making a tilt at a top four spot seem more wearisome than a 1974 episode of 'Emmerdale Farm' (the hardcore days, before they dropped the 'Farm' from its name and filled the soap with rutting teenage eye-candy). Allardyce resigned from his position at Bolton with two games of the 2006–07 season remaining and hasn't been heard of since.

With the start of the season looming, and finding himself fast running out of options, Niall Quinn appointed Niall Quinn as temporary team manager after first getting the go-ahead from the rest of the consortium. He said, 'My job is to get us to turn the corner and get us into a position where we can attract the world class manager we want. It could take three months, twelve months, 18 months, I don't know.'

It wasn't Quinn's first spell as Sunderland manager – he unofficially did the job for a few days after Peter Reid was sacked in 2002 after a shocking run of five wins in 28 games. After those few days, and without the Irishman actually getting the chance to preside over a match, Howard Wilkinson arrived at the Stadium of Light and things quickly got much, much, much, much worse.

Quinn's first act as boss in 2006 was to bring Bobby Saxton back to the club. Saxton had been Reid's loyal assistant and had left a few months before Reid himself got the axe. Quinn was quick to sing the praises of his new sidekick's earlier achievements with the Black Cats, saying, 'Bobby Saxton was instrumental in bringing this club to where it went seven or eight years ago. Sometimes the chairman or the manager gets all the credit, but ask the people in-house who was responsible and they will say it was Bobby.'

Saxton was charged with the task of bringing some buoyancy back to the dressing room and coaxing some attacking play out of a group of shell-shocked players who had grown into the habit of being easy prey for opposition over the previous season.

With Quinn easing his giant frame into the manager's chair, the overriding air of optimism that had swathed the city following the Drumaville takeover took further hold. Hindsight and a quick look at Quinn's mercifully short managerial record shows that such optimism was at best naïve, but if you're hanging over a cliff edge by a tuft of grass and someone hands you a greasy rope, you'd be mad not to make a grab for it.

Quinn will never be a successful football manager – for one thing, it isn't something he wants to do, and he took the reins at Sunderland almost out of desperation when another suitable candidate failed to materialise. The new boss told supporters that he was happy to play a waiting game in order to recruit the right man for the job, a 'world class manager.'

Five straight defeats later and with the club anchored to the bottom of the Coca-Cola Championship, the need for such a manager to come in and sort things out couldn't have been more urgent. A 2-0 reverse at Bury in the Carling Cup was the last straw. Bury went into the match rock-bottom of the Football League and their comfortable win led to the unusual spectacle of a visibly frustrated Quinn announcing that he would soon be sacking himself as team manager, while revealing that there was a 70/30 chance of bringing in a world class manager in the following few days.

The defeat at Bury was one of those wretched low points that for Sunderland fans are as inevitable as death, taxes and getting cheap laughs from the maelstrom of ego-fuelled blundering up the road at St James' Park. For newer fans of Sunderland, in a footballing sense, Bury was probably the lowest point ever. Older supporters have their own versions of 'SAFC Ground Zero', those days when the club's plight (almost always self-inflicted) leads to tightness in the chest and cold sweat running down the back. Times when thoughts turn to abandoning football-supporting as a lifestyle choice and turning to milder pursuits like parachuting, tattooing your own tongue or acquiring an expensive and destructive drug habit.

So, post-Bury, and with the team in absolute free-fall, the hunt for a new manager was underway again. The field was considerably narrower this time around following

Quinn's assertion that a 'world class' manager would be taking over. Obviously, this ruled out some of the previously mooted names like the freshly unemployed and vaguely creepy ex-Aston Villa boss David O'Leary.

But what was the chairman's definition of 'world class'? Glenn Hoddle? Surely not. Alan Curbishley, holidaying after a decade of doing-okay-I-suppose with Charlton Athletic? Both men were without jobs but you could hardly cast them as players on the global stage, even with Hoddle's queasy, slightly psychedelic tenure as England manager taken into consideration.

Sam Allardyce's name had been wheeled into the frame yet again a few days earlier, but dedicated, hardcore followers of rumour and gossip were tiring of the links with Big Sam and were searching for fresh managerial meat to hunt. In fact it had emerged that Allardyce was allegedly happy for his name to be linked with the job as a method of securing extra transfer funds from his chairman at Bolton, a tactic he had reportedly used before. Then, just as fans were readying themselves for another drawn-out, nail-biting spell of speculation, Chinese whispers and good old-fashioned lies, Richard Keys delivered the news like a bolt from the blue. Roy Keane. The new 'world class' manager of Sunderland AFC.

For Keane, the opportunity at Sunderland presented him with his first challenge in the bear-pit of club management and, given the size and potential of the club coupled with the ambition of the new owners, a decidedly tasty one. His arrival on Wearside was as unexpected as his departure from Manchester United had been.

Thirteen years of almost unremitting success at Old Trafford, with a large chunk of that time spent as club captain, came to a swift and shocking end when a furious and disillusioned Keane railed against the deficiencies of his team-mates on the club's official TV station after a 4-1 defeat at the hands of Middlesbrough. Within days he was gone – the season which was intended to be his swansong had been cut short and Keane left by the back door.

An indifferent few months followed playing for his boyhood idols Celtic, during which he collected the final two medals of his playing career, but age and a creaking hip finally caught up with him and he announced his retirement in June 2006. Two months later and the extended break that he had planned from the game was cut short – he was at Sunderland.

He later spoke of the careful deliberation he gave to the opportunity of taking over the Black Cats, particularly when a concerned relative called him after the Bury defeat and said, 'Roy, I think you should take the Sunderland job – Niall's just been on television and he looks like he's about to have a heart attack'. Keane thought for a moment before replying, 'Perhaps I should give it another week then.'

But as the story broke unofficially, behind the scenes a deal was being struck. For once, Niall Quinn was keeping his cards close to his chest, angrily dismissing the Richard Keys announcement, insisting that nothing had been confirmed and seeming annoyed and frustrated at further needless speculation. A few days later though, and what was the game's worst-kept-secret was confirmed as Keane was officially named as the next Sunderland manager.

The appointment caught out almost everyone in football. In the press, masses of column inches were devoted to speculation over whether the 'volatile Irishman' (© most journalists) possessed what it takes to be a successful manager. The majority were quick to prejudge Keane unfavourably and assume that the lazy, cartoonish image he'd acquired as a bulging-veined maniac midfielder would be the one he would carry into the more sophisticated realm of club management. Those who had watched Keane play towards the end of his career should have noted that a significant amount of restraint had been added to his game as the years caught up with him, which took little away from his effectiveness as a player and captain.

However, with that in mind it could well have been this shift in the way he expressed himself that led him to bottle up his demons and provoke the outburst aimed at his team-mates which hurried his departure from Old Trafford.

Liberal amounts of fire and brimstone for Keane and Sunderland were being forecast in the press. In *The Times*, Simon Barnes wrote, 'I fear the rage will win, that the rows, the feuds, the walking-outs will outnumber the triumphs.' The *Observer's* Paul Wilson was similarly gloomy, opining, 'The problem is that Keane might be temperamentally unsuited to management. At times in the past few years he has appeared barely in control of himself, let alone capable of bringing out the best in others.

James Lawton of *The Independent* was keener to see the possibility of hidden dimensions to Keane's character, writing, 'The winning managers know, from the start, that they have to change; they have to acquire cunning, if not instant wisdom, but more important than anything they have to understand that what they demanded from themselves was a burden they alone knew they could carry.'

Lawton was right – too many top players had failed to transform themselves into successful managers by failing to realise that they were dealing with far less talented players than they themselves had been.

The piece rightly noted that Keane's two dominant managerial influences had been Brian Clough and Sir Alex Ferguson – hardly the worst tutors in the management game.

Once Keane's imminent appointment had been confirmed, he pitched up at the Stadium of Light to witness Quinn's farewell match as manager, a coronation filled with renewed optimism, even if the attendance of 24,242 for a Bank Holiday Monday match suggested that there was still some work to be done coaxing vexed fans back to the Stadium of Light.

Inspired by the arrival of Keane, Sunderland's bedraggled players suddenly found what was required to get a win, comfortably beating West Bromwich Albion by two goals to nil, and seemed a tidier, more confident unit than the one that had stumbled blindly into the Championship season, oozing negativity and leaking late goals. The fact that Roy Keane was glaring down at the team from his vantage point in the directors' box may or may not have been significant.

The new manager declined to sign his contract before the match only because he would have felt the need to take charge if he had, and as Quinn had already announced the line-up to the players, it was felt that this would be inappropriate. But Keane had been introduced to the players the day before the West Brom match and Quinn later said, 'He brought a buzz to the place. When Roy met the players, you could almost see them standing an inch or two taller.'

Even as Keane and Quinn took their seats for the press conference the day after the West Brom win, no-one could be entirely sure who Sunderland were really getting. Perhaps the whole thing was actually some kind of elaborate ploy which Keane had dreamt up, aimed at getting revenge against Quinn for the infamous fall-out in Saipan in 2002, when he stormed out of Ireland's World Cup camp, heading for home and dissolving his rage with some intensive dog-walking.

After the way Keane had turned on his team-mates at Manchester United just a few months earlier, it might have been perfectly reasonable to assume that he had gone insane and would walk into the press conference, rip up his freshly-inked contract, throw the pieces in Quinn's face and roar, 'That's for not backing me up in Saipan you giant bastard.'

Thankfully, that didn't happen and Keane faced the cameras carrying no visible weaponry; plus the absence of dried blood around his mouth suggested that he hadn't recently feasted on any helpless animals or slain any of what was popularly imagined to be his many enemies. Instead it was a charming, calm and measured man who was introduced to the press, and Keane comfortably batted away provocative questions with no trace of aggression towards his inquisitors.

In fact it was the journalists who were on the front foot, probing for any evidence of lingering ill-feeling between the employer and his new employee. As Quinn and Keane were once equals and had barely spoken to one another for four years, this was fair game, but the hacks phrased their questions with extreme care.

Although the chances were slim, the fear still lingered that one ill-chosen question could cause Keane to bound over the table and charge into the crowd, windmilling his fists at all and sundry before storming out and walking his dog furiously along the bank of the Wear.

The fact that the chairman and his new manager were even sitting beside one another and united by the same cause was bizarre enough – in his autobiography Keane had depicted Quinn as a 'muppet' and a 'coward', while Quinn hadn't exactly endeared himself to his former international colleague by once saying, 'If Roy buttered his toast it would have to be perfect.'

No matter – it was established in a matter of moments that what had gone on in 2002 was dead and buried. 'That was discussed when we first met,' said Keane. 'If you are going to beat about the bush and ask, "Did I apologise?" – of course I did. But it wasn't a case of apologising to get a job. Far from it. I don't think I was that desperate or ever will be.'

It emerged that the pair had buried the hatchet months previously and this had been Quinn's second approach to Keane for the manager's job ('He interviewed us', the chairman joked) and after originally turning down the job in favour of completing his UEFA coaching badges, Keane revealed that his decision had taken him all of ten seconds this time around ('I thought, "What am I waiting for?" Big club, beautiful stadium, big fanbase – Why not?').

He also spelled out what he'd be expecting from the dilapidated squad he'd be inheriting, his simplistic message being, 'If they give one hundred per cent to Sunderland there will not be a problem but if they take their eye off the ball there will be. It's very straightforward.' Simplistic his message might have been, but it was laced with a very real threat that said 'shape up or ship out.'

Despite having pledged to bring in a world class boss and then actually delivering a rookie, the rookie chairman himself was delighted with the acquisition of Keane, declaring it, 'a statement of intent from the people of Drumaville.' Quinn added that his new manager, 'brings to the table everything to lift this club to where I think it should be.'

The magic carpet was now ready for take-off.

CHAPTER TWO

HOW LOW CAN YOU GO?

SUNDERLAND'S 2006–07 SEASON began with the same fixture as in the Championship-winning campaign two years before, away at Coventry City. The Sky Blues were now residing at their new home, the Ricoh Arena, another of the epidemic of purpose-built identikit football stadia that are slowly draining the individualism and heart from British football.

Helpfully, the stadium is also located in the middle of nowhere. Coventry took the points in the opening fixture two years before, but the Black Cats went on to take the Championship title that season. With the momentum of the Drumaville takeover, a better start was expected this time.

For the past 30 years, older and wearier Sunderland fans have viewed the Sky Blues with withering contempt, stemming from the suspicious activities during the final game of the 1976–77 season. On that day, Sunderland were away at Everton while Coventry played host to Bristol City. A run of results worthy of European qualification had seen the Wearsiders clamber to the brink of safety and a win at Everton would guarantee top-flight status. The only other teams who could go down were... Coventry and Bristol City. Whoever lost in their match would be relegated.

Somehow, possibly at the behest of Coventry's chairman Jimmy Hill, the match at Highfield Road kicked off later than the one at Goodison. Everton duly beat Sunderland 2-0, which meant that if Coventry v Bristol City ended in a draw, they would both survive. With three minutes still to play at Coventry, news of Sunderland's defeat came through, and as if by magic, what had been a keenly-fought 2-2 draw suddenly dissolved into a gentle kickabout, with neither side willing to take any needless risks that could relegate them. No FA charges were brought and nothing was ever proven, but if indeed there was some underhand activity, all of those involved will surely perish in hell. Imagine it if you can – an eternity of damnation alongside Jimmy Hill. It's not a pretty thought.

Tension between the two clubs erupted into on-pitch violence in 1990 when Sunderland skipper Gary Bennett got embroiled in a touchline dust-up with Coventry's deeply annoying striker David Speedie. The altercation ended with Bennett grabbing Speedie by the throat and pushing him over the advertising hoardings into the Clock Stand.

Bennett later recalled the incident with fondness, saying, 'he ended up in the crowd but they just kept pushing him back. When supporters ask me about David Speedie I always tell them, "It's your fault, you lot could have sorted him out once and for all that night!"'

In more recent years, meetings between the two clubs saw horrific injuries inflicted on Coventry's Stephen Froggatt and Sunderland's Colin Healy. It speaks volumes for the pull of the Sky Blues that when defender Phil Babb ended his jaw-grindingly mediocre time with Sunderland and was offered the chance to return to Coventry City for a second spell, he opted instead to retire altogether from the game and launch a new career running a struggling golf magazine.

Back in 2006 and with the newly-signed veteran Kenny Cunningham as the only red and white debutant, Sunderland's reluctant manager Niall Quinn knew that he had to somehow fashion a side that might be capable of getting in and among the scuffle for promotion. In truth, there was no real reason why, given a good start, they couldn't string a few results together and get a foothold in that leading pack.

After all, the heart of the side that started the 2006–07 season, players like Stephen Caldwell, Danny Collins, Dean Whitehead, Liam Lawrence and Stephen Elliott had all played a huge part in the 2004 Championship win. If they could reboot themselves as players, shut out the horrors of the past year and channel the spirit that had so efficiently got the job done two years before, they should be easily capable of doing it again.

Sadly, the message that the 2,500 fans who made the trip to Coventry in 2006 got was that a losing mentality had become as much a part of Sunderland's identity as the red and white stripes themselves.

Sunderland started vigorously despite the blazing sunshine, conditions which weren't helped by a 1.30pm kick-off dictated by Sky Sports. For an away side, they looked well-organised, spirited, and keen to probe their opponents' final third in search of an opening goal. As the half progressed, Coventry regrouped and began to find their feet, but Sunderland had good reason to be satisfied with their performance by the time the interval arrived. Granted, there was the odd comedic throwback to the previous season's travails – the sight of two Sunderland defenders challenging each other for the ball, and neither of them actually winning it, acted as a swift reminder for anyone who thought that the horrors of the previous season had been forgotten.

If they could sustain their momentum in the second period, a point or perhaps all three were surely there for the taking, and indeed it was Sunderland who opened the scoring in the 52nd minute. While he had been goal-shy in the Premiership, Daryl Murphy had gone on a pre-season spree against lower league opposition and his run continued as he stabbed the ball home from six yards out after Coventry failed to clear a corner. A blatant handball was missed or deliberately ignored by the referee and Elliott cleverly hooked it into the danger area where it fell to Murphy to get Sunderland off the mark for the new season.

Now was the time to take hold of the game – to be strong and press for a second goal while remaining diligent in defence. Unfortunately, it never happened. Coventry knew an equaliser was there for the taking if they continued to stick to the tactics with which they had ended the first half. Sunderland's players began to wilt visibly and it wasn't just down to the heat. The team that had performed so catastrophically on the field throughout the previous season had needed leadership and direction for far longer than the fortnight or so that Quinn had allowed himself and Bobby Saxton to mould it into their desired shape.

The inevitable equaliser came in the 71st minute with the strong, purposeful Stern John receiving the ball with his back to goal, turning away from Kenny Cunningham and working an angle before lofting it into the far corner beyond Ben Alnwick's reach. It was a rare moment of genuine quality in the match and it sealed Sunderland's fate. By now the Black Cats were bereft of ideas as well as belief and it was a case of when rather than if Coventry would finish off the job.

The winning goal was so riddled with defensive incompetence that it should belong on a coaching course – on a DVD to be shown at the beginning by way of bringing some light relief to the proceedings. Conceding a foul on the left-hand touchline, Sunderland's players began trotting amiably into their positions as Coventry tried to exploit the situation with a quick free-kick, releasing Gary McSheffrey unmarked into the penalty box. Fortunately, referee Chris Foy whistled to allow himself to catch up with play before the Sky Blues re-took the kick. They did this in exactly the same way again, Sunderland still seemingly oblivious to the impending threat as McSheffrey was allowed to ghost into the box unchallenged and drill a deflected shot through a gang of jelly-legged 'defenders.'

So one game gone and one defeat, but at least Sunderland's failings were there for all to see. Quinn described Coventry's winner as a 'giveaway goal', calling it, 'a little glitch that's in there that I've got to get out very, very quickly. It's intelligence and it's professionalism and we have to get it sorted.'

Whether they could iron out that glitch in time for the arrival at the Stadium of Light of promotion favourites Birmingham City would remain to be seen.

Off the field, Quinn continued his frantic attempts to recruit extra players with sufficient quality to lift the side, stating his intentions to have two players fighting for every position by the closure of the transfer window at the end of August.

Barcelona's B-team captain Arnau Rirea arrived on a free transfer but an exciting young striker by the name of Anthony Stokes was deemed unsuitable following a brief trial period at the Academy of Light and was sent back to Arsenal. Another significant bit of business was completed as the injured George McCartney signed for

West Ham, passing the Hammers' left-back Clive Clarke on the motorway as he headed in the opposite direction to the Stadium of Light. McCartney followed Julio Arca out of the club; the popular Argentine midfielder had departed for Middlesbrough, seemingly disorientated from not knowing which league he was playing in following a string of promotions and relegations with Sunderland.

Reports suggested that the boss was setting his transfer sights high with bids placed for three Premiership players. Among those was Aston Villa's Kevin Phillips, undoubtedly Sunderland's best player over the past quarter of a century, scoring 131 goals in just 234 appearances, breaking the club's post-war scoring record and winning the European Golden Boot award along the way. But fans were divided over whether 'Super Kev' should return – players rarely do as well during a second spell at a club, although it would be hard for Phillips to do any better. Even though he hadn't been as prolific since leaving Sunderland for Southampton and then Villa, he had still consistently scored goals and there would be no doubt that he would be up to the job in the Championship.

It was with the Super Kev speculation buzzing in the air that Quinn's side faced Birmingham City for the season's first match at the Stadium of Light. The link to a player with Phillips' undeniable quality had given the supporters a lift, even though at this stage it remained just speculation. Additionally, although Quinn had hoped for a crowd of around 35,000 for the home take-off of his 'magic carpet ride', the actual turn-out was a disappointing three-quarters of that figure and a 1-0 defeat was about all that Sunderland deserved.

It was an evening where the inevitability of defeat lingered in the air from fairly early on – Sunderland's players worked hard in every area of the pitch, but there was still no visible progression from the previous weekend or the previous season. Sheer graft will never win much on a football field unless it's married to some spark of inspiration, and although Sunderland certainly grafted against Birmingham, and were always looking to conjure up a decisive attacking move, their efforts stalled in the final third too many times, and that killer pass that opens up opposition defences was never there on a frustrating August evening.

Sunderland were forced to shuffle things around at the back when Steven Caldwell limped out of the match to be replaced by new signing Clive Clarke, who filled in at left-back with Danny Collins switching to the middle. Any goodwill from the home fans towards debutant Clarke quickly evaporated when he gifted Birmingham the lead within ten minutes of coming on. His sluggish challenge on Damien Johnson in the box looked like the sort of tackle you'd expect to see from a striker and the appeals were half-hearted when the referee awarded the penalty, which Mikel Forsell stroked well out of Ben Alnwick's reach into the corner of the net.

Sunderland had the ball in the net three minutes later when Liam Lawrence curled a right-foot past Maik Taylor, but the referee quickly cancelled out the equaliser, judging that the offside Daryl Murphy had got a glancing touch to the ball on its way in. It was the only bright spot of a shocking performance from Lawrence, who looked uncomfortable stationed on the left flank, and whose body language rarely showed that he was capable or willing to adjust to his new position.

After the disallowed goal it was never going to be Sunderland's night, and the Midlanders were content to let Sunderland play their way into trouble, looking to exploit the counter-attack when the gaps inevitably opened up in the Wearsiders' defence. The life slowly drained out of the game and by the end, expectation had yet again turned to disappointment for the hardcore red and white supporters. The all-new, gung-ho attacking style of play which Quinn had promised failed to appear, and Sunderland looked as bereft of quality in this league as they had done in the top flight the season before. Something needed to happen to stop the rot. Bring on St Niall's Day!

Coinciding with the following Saturday's home match and promoted by the leading Sunderland fanzine *A Love Supreme*, St Niall's Day was billed as an opportunity for fans to give thanks to Quinn for saving the club by draping themselves in Irish green and drowning themselves in Guinness. Some later said that it might have been worth querying the wisdom of holding the event on a day when the visitors were a side who play in green.

In the end, a collective depression brought on by the season's start meant it was a damp squib, with the majority of green shirts in the ground being worn by the away fans. With their long and arduous trek to the north east, the Plymouth Argyle supporters justified their nickname of The Pilgrims – in fact it might have been an easier trip for them if they were playing away against Espanyol or Galatasaray.

St Niall's Day got off to the best possible start with less than half a minute on the clock when Daryl Murphy, controlling a hopeful forward ball and holding off a defender, drilled the ball home with his left foot. Quinn came racing out of his dugout to the touchline to celebrate this perfect opening – perhaps it was time for Sunderland to finally kick-start their season after two false starts. However, the party atmosphere lasted for roughly seven minutes until normal service was resumed when David Norris broke into the right-hand side of the Sunderland box and hit a looping shot over Ben Alnwick, whose positioning was dubious to say the least. If the 'keeper had been a couple of feet closer to his goal line, he could have comfortably tipped the ball to safety. Alnwick was already beginning to show signs of shell-shock brought about by being the last line of defence in a team crippled by a lack of confidence.

Worse came just before half-time – Kenny Cunningham underhit a back-pass to Alnwick allowing Plymouth's Barry Hayles to pick up the ball in no man's land and stab it efficiently toward the empty net, via the head of the hapless Danny Collins.

The party was in danger of turning into a wake and there was precious little to celebrate in the second half, with Sunderland continuing to attack but without any real creativity, pace or guile. But they kept plugging away, and when Daryl Murphy broke down the left-hand side in the 68th minute, he was able to loft a cross over to the back post, finding Stephen Elliott in a pocket of space he'd found six yards from goal. Elliott, undoubtedly the side's natural goal-poacher, made no mistake. Two-all.

The momentum was swinging back towards the Black Cats and in the following few minutes Chris Brown and Daryl Murphy both had excellent chances to give Sunderland the lead. Both were denied by Plymouth's 'keeper, Luke McCormick, who pulled off a couple of magnificent fingertip saves. Despite Sunderland's best efforts, the luck of the Irish seemed to be somewhere else on St Niall's Day.

As at Coventry and against Birmingham, there was an awful sense of inevitability about the outcome of the match. The decisive moment was yet another example of Sunderland's ability to commit defensive suicide in moments when there appeared to be no real danger. Danny Collins (enjoying another annoyingly ineffective run-out) failed to deal with a hopeful through ball from Plymouth's half.

After committing the cardinal sin of letting it bounce, Collins then fell on his backside as Nick Chadwick bundled him off the ball and headed off towards goal. Beating the shattered Alnwick was a formality and Sunderland were behind again.

The Wearsiders had a chance to draw level in the dying minutes but Chris Brown hit a weak shot straight at McCormick. A 3-2 defeat. The third in seven days, and one which left the team languishing in 21st place in the league table. The only relief was that statistics showed they were only the fourth worst team at this point. St Niall had seen enough, saying, 'after that, only the tough will survive. It was the good, the bad and the ugly of Sunderland Football Club.'

He vowed to root out those who did not have the backbone to compete and play with complete heart and soul, adding, 'everyone who was at that match today – and their dog – would know we need to freshen it up with new faces.' You know you're in trouble when even the dogs can spot what's wrong...

The need to bring players into the squad who were free of a losing mentality was growing more urgent, with just three weeks remaining until the transfer window would slam closed for its four-month break. The Kevin Phillips saga rumbled on, as new Aston Villa manager Martin O'Neill took time to assess his squad and decide who would stay and who would go.

A major offer had also been made to Tottenham for their Irish left-winger Andy Reid, and such was Quinn's determination to land the Irish winger that he twice increased his bid. In the end, Reid wasn't prepared to drop down a level – not immediately anyway, opting instead to join Charlton Athletic, who would go on to find themselves relegated at the end of the season. Phillips and Reid were among five players for whom Quinn revealed he had placed bids.

Another week on the training field had failed to heal the psychological wounds that had hung over from the Premiership and infested the start of the new season. A 3-1 defeat at Southend United on August 19th maintained Sunderland's 100% losing start and saw the patience of the manager and the travelling supporters stretched to the limit.

Supporters turned on the players with chants of 'You're not fit to wear the shirt', while a handful went further, throwing their shirts at the players in disgust. A goal on the stroke of half-time by Southend defender Adam Barrett had served as a huge blow for Sunderland and after the interval the team rolled over once again. Barrett added a second before Lee Bradbury made it 3-0 with a couple of minutes remaining.

Jon Stead saved his best for last, capping a diabolical personal performance with a last-minute consolation goal, if consolation is the right word.

Stead had been one of Mick McCarthy's more curious buys a year before, snapping him up from Blackburn Rovers where he had scored just twice in 29 attempts during the previous season. Perhaps McCarthy had some kind of remarkable insight and had seen something that other observers of the game had missed. Perhaps not – Stead's goal at Southend would be his second and final strike for the club in 40 appearances accumulated for the Black Cats before his eventual departure to Sheffield United. If, as his body language always suggested, he was a player who thrived on confidence, Jon Stead had made a huge mistake in coming to Sunderland.

By now the team were in danger of plummeting down through the Championship and straight into League One – the old Third Division! – and the reason was a mystery to no one. After Southend, Quinn said, 'I think this was the day when we realised for sure that there is a percentage of them who are not good enough. On the training ground everything seems fine but in matches, this fear, this losing mentality that is rampant in our dressing room undoes us all the time.'

The supporters had already decided who the players were that weren't showing the required heart needed to turn the situation around. The aforementioned Stead was joined on the fans' hit list by Liam Lawrence, Danny Collins, and Rory Delap.

Ben Alnwick was being excused, mostly because local players traditionally get an easier ride from Sunderland fans – in the past forwards like Craig Russell and Michael Proctor were lauded as being far better players than they ever were, mostly due to their place of birth. In truth, Alnwick's positioning and kicking had been continually poor, and although he'd just signed a new four year contract, he would need to show significant improvement if he wanted to hold on to the 'keeper's shirt at the club.

There was to be no improvement whatsoever at Bury in the Coca-Cola Cup three days later. Many of the fans making their way to the ground would have been heartened by memories of their last trip to Gigg Lane in 1999, when Sunderland won 5-2 to clinch promotion to the Premiership, a certain Kevin Phillips scoring four of those goals. Fast forward to 2006 and, just before kick-off, the surprising news broke that Phillips had opted to stay in the Midlands and sign for West

Bromwich Albion. Officially, he later said that he had been unwilling to uproot his young family and return to the north east for a second spell, although a quick look at the league table can't have made the decision any tougher for him.

Amazingly, out of a crowd of 2,390 at Gigg Lane, around 1,200 were Sunderland supporters. Many of them were probably still finding their seats as Arnau was sent off in the third minute for the use of an elbow. A story later circulated that Niall Quinn had asked for the away dressing room to be locked after the players headed out on to the pitch. When the Bury official returned with the key, one player had been left behind in full kit. 'I been sent off' he mumbled in broken English.

So, right from the off, the Wearsiders were up against it again. Although Bury were anchored to the bottom of League Two, this was potentially a major scalp for them and the red card gave them a platform to build upon. Sunderland meanwhile, were showing admirable consistency – yet again they huffed and puffed around the field but were toothless up front.

Daryl Murphy looked a long way from adding to the two goals he'd scored earlier in the month, while Stephen Elliott was still desperately scrabbling for some kind of form and looking a pale shadow of the player who had scored for fun in the Championship two years previously.

The game dragged on, devoid of any real quality from either side, until Sunderland's fatigue from being a man short finally started to tell, Bury taking the lead in the 83rd minute with a free header from defender John Fitzgerald. He celebrated by leaping into the crowd and as he'd already been booked, it was to be his last act of the evening. A second yellow card was duly whipped out by the referee and Fitzgerald followed Arnau down the tunnel.

The levelling of numbers came too late for Sunderland to get anything from the game and Bury hammered another nail in the coffin with three minutes to go. The Sunderland defence seemed to think the game had ended when Andy Bishop raced through and lifted the ball past Alnwick to wrap the result up.

Afterwards Niall Quinn faced the media, visibly distraught by the result and another performance that was so far away from an acceptable level as to be scarcely believable. The optimism and hope that surrounded the takeover by Quinn and his Drumaville consortium had led to one of Sunderland's worst starts in living memory. The manager who'd never wanted the job was quitting. A world class boss was on his way.

CHAPTER THREE

CHILDREN OF THE ROYVOLUTION

AS A PLAYER, Roy Keane's last act at the Stadium of Light had been to swing an elbow at his Irish team-mate and Sunderland midfielder Jason McAteer. It happened in the final minute of a 1-1 draw in August 2002 – referee Uriah Rennie wasted no time in whipping out the red card and Keane slowly made his way towards the touchline. Never afraid to escalate a tense situation with some mickey-taking, McAteer recovered in time to mime a gesture of writing in a notebook to the Irish captain, suggesting to the 47,500 crowd that Keane might want to include the incident in his next book.

As the sense of theatre increased, Niall Quinn also trotted over to Keane, offering an outstretched hand in an attempt to broker peace following their fall-out during that summer's World Cup in Saipan. Not surprisingly, Keane wasn't in the mood for buddying up at that point in time.

The Irishman's next appearance at the Stadium of Light was just as notable, but far more significant for Sunderland fans. By now, Roy Keane and Niall Quinn had settled their differences, which was probably for the best if Keane was to manage the club of which Quinn was now the chairman. Although he was yet to officially sign his contract and take over, Keane took his seat for the Bank Holiday Monday visit of West Bromwich Albion and had briefly met the players beforehand.

The Keane effect worked immediately; Sunderland looked like a more focused unit when going forward and finally collected their first points of the season. Dean Whitehead scored a freak opening goal on 33 minutes when his corner from the left-hand side floated over both attackers and defenders and crossed the line before a West Brom defender could hack it away.

The Black Cats' second goal came just after half-time – Neill Collins heading in Tobias Hysen's well-taken free-kick. Although they were among the promotion favourites, West Brom were never at the races and the day became an unofficial coronation for the new boss. Even the booing of Kevin Phillips, who came on as a second half sub for his new side, soon petered out when the Wearside crowd realised his role as a potential villain wasn't going to affect the game's outcome.

With under 25,000 in the ground, the attendance was low, but the match was broadcast live on Sky, and it has to be remembered that it was only Sunderland's third league victory in 24 attempts for 2006 – at this stage thousands of fans were instead choosing to spend match days curled up in a ball in a darkened corner somewhere, quietly weeping.

Those who were there or saw it on TV witnessed a transformed side. Perhaps the training ground work of Quinn and Saxton was starting to bear fruit, but the improvement was not insignificantly due to the arrival of Keane. Niall Quinn had spoken of the squad being introduced to the new manager and the players standing taller and thinking "we are going to be working with that man".' They all knew what he stood for as a player, and for each and every one of them it was going to be sink or swim from then on.

Keane wasted no time in strengthening the worn out squad he had inherited, while at the same time stressing that every player at the club would start with a clean slate under his reign. He had little time to act as the transfer window was due to close just over 48 hours after he took charge, and he wisely recruited players who he knew.

He returned to his last club, Celtic, recruiting left-winger Ross Wallace and defender Stanislav Varga, who would begin his second spell as a Sunderland player. From Manchester United came Liam Miller, hailed by some as 'the new Keane' when he arrived at Old Trafford from Celtic in 2004, but who had spent the previous season on loan at Leeds, and was well accustomed to the unique charms of Championship football.

Keane also enrolled two former international colleagues, Graham Kavanagh and David Connolly, both heading to Wearside from Wigan. Connolly had impressed Keane on past international trips with Ireland with his desire to spend his spare time working in the gym instead of lounging around or playing golf.

The most eye-catching of all the signings was that of Dwight Yorke; impish striker, international playboy and a team-mate of Keane's in the 1999 treble-winning side at Old Trafford.

The pair were as unlike each other as any two footballers could be. Keane was the broody, insular perfectionist who hadn't been born with the greatest footballing talent but had become one of the dominant players of his generation through a mixture of education and application. Yorke, meanwhile, was a naturally gifted forward who, although it almost sounds like a cliché, always played with a smile on his face.

Yorke's career had more or less peaked following the

treble season and Keane brought him back to English football following a season playing on the other side of the world for Sydney FC under former Wearside hate-figure Terry Butcher. For Keane to recruit him was an immediate sign that there would plenty of room for flair in the new-look Sunderland.

Due to an international break in the domestic schedule, the old and the new would have just over a week together to gel before taking to the field for the first time, away at Derby County's Pride Park. There was something fitting about the fact that Keane and Sunderland would have to travel down Brian Clough Way, as the A52 had been renamed in honour of the man who had cast such an influence over Keane, Sunderland and Derby County. Five thousand rejuvenated Sunderland fans made the journey down the same road – the response to the Roy Keane appointment had been overwhelmingly positive.

Before Keane had even taken the job, Ladbrokes were offering 5/2 against him leaving Sunderland before Christmas, so strong was the feeling that his volcanic temperament would lead to his speedy downfall as a manager. But ahead of the Derby game, the new manager showed more of the dry sense of humour he had displayed at the press conference announcing his appointment, when he was asked if he'd received any good luck messages ahead of his managerial debut? 'Yeah, zero. My wife wished me well, but that's because she's not seen me for two weeks. Otherwise I've had none, so I'll be waiting by the fax.'

Five of the manager's new signings started the match, with only Dwight Yorke missing as he had only arrived in the UK the previous day. As the game kicked off, the Black Cats were utterly unrecognisable from the dejected mob who had sloped off the pitch at Southend and Bury a few short weeks before. Pride Park was a fitting name for the debut of this new-look Sunderland as they tore into Derby from the first whistle.

At times their first-half display was more about noise and chaos than anything else and once the game settled down, Derby began to impose themselves more and more, with Sunderland's familiar defensive uncertainties flaring up again. The Rams deserved their half-time lead, Matt Oakley crashing the ball home from a knock-down by Sunderland-born Steve Howard right on the stroke of half-time.

Although they went in a goal behind, there was no ranting and raving in the dressing room. 'I told them to trust each other and things would be all right,' Keane said afterwards, and in fact sent the players out for the second half five minutes ahead of the kick-off. It was an impressive early deployment of the kind of mind-games that Alex Ferguson had mastered at Manchester United, and the softly softly approach did the trick.

On 62 minutes, Graham Kavanagh orchestrated a one-two down the left-hand side before easing the ball into the six-yard area. Chris Brown eventually connected with it and scrambled it over the line before leaping into the frenzied crowd of Sunderland fans behind the goal, earning himself a yellow card.

It was a scrappy piece of forward play but no matter; Sunderland were level and in a position to try and take the game to Derby; in fact the Black Cats took the lead less than two minutes later. The visitors continued to press forward following Brown's goal, and Derby's defence were caught napping as Ross Wallace nudged the ball into a yard of space before drilling it home from 20 yards with his left foot. Keane was out of his dugout, punching the air.

After Sunderland took the lead, Derby wilted and

couldn't find a way back into the match as Sunderland held on for their lives. Any hopes held out by more cynical observers that Keane would spend the 90 minutes at Derby launching volleys of abuse at the officials or bawling orders at his players until the veins in his temples exploded were dashed.

For the most part he was calmness personified, becoming only slightly agitated as the second half reached its climax, particularly when the referee somehow found another five minutes to add on at the end before Keane sealed his winning start. Two wins on the bounce for the team, and a sign of some gathering momentum. However, the fact remained that the team still lacked the composure required to take control of matches and dominate their way to victory. It took them another four days and a trip to Elland Road to get the hang of that.

Prior to Sunderland's arrival, seven of Leeds' eight league games had been decided with a single goal. Unfortunately for Leeds, match nine wasn't going to be as tight as that. The ailing Yorkshire giants had struggled to score goals all season and their few attacking efforts were ably dealt with by the Wearsiders, who put on a supremely confident display and ravaged their opponents, wrapping the game up just after half-time as Stephen Elliott smacked a shot past Tony Warner from the right-hand side of the penalty area.

Liam Miller, coming up against the club he had represented the previous year, had opened the scoring after 28 minutes with a shot that crawled and bobbled along the ground on its way past the 'keeper, while Sunderland's second was a first-time shot hit across the 'keeper from 20 yards out by Graham Kavanagh. Three nil, with three goals scored by three Irishmen.

Keane wasn't surprised, saying afterwards, 'The fact

is, I'm coming to Leeds expecting to win, so I'm not sitting here afterwards in a state of shock.'

On the night there was more aggression from the Leeds fans than there was from their team. There's never been any love lost between fans of Sunderland and Leeds, or fans of Leeds and anyone else for that matter. Back in 1973, the Yorkshire club were regarded by many as the best team in the country, but were humiliated in the FA Cup Final when they were expected to steamroller over the Second Division minnows from Wearside. Sunderland fans celebrated that historical 1-0 win by carrying a white coffin around the pitch at Roker Park a few days later with 'Leeds Died 1973' painted on both sides.

The animosity has continued ever since and trouble flared outside the ground after the match, with windows smashed on coaches carrying Sunderland supporters. Inside the ground, a pair of Leeds fans tried to get at Roy Keane moments before the start of the second half. Stewards arrived in time to intercept them and defuse what could have been a nasty incident, but Keane was quick to brush it off, quipping, 'I just thought the fans got lost.'

The Leeds 'supporters' would shame themselves further at the end of the season when hundreds of them invaded the Elland Road pitch with seconds remaining of the match that was to condemn them to relegation. It would be the first time that the club had dropped into the league's third tier, coming just six years after they appeared in a Champions League semi-final and following a period of horrendous financial mismanagement. Sunderland fans could be forgiven for thinking how close the Black Cats might have come to following them, if Niall Quinn and Drumaville hadn't intervened.

In the aftermath, Sunderland's injury worries increased, with Stephen Elliott ruled out for up to two months with ankle ligament damage picked up at Leeds. David Connolly would also be ruled out of the next match, which would mean Dwight Yorke would be in line to make his debut in Roy Keane's first home match as manager against Leicester City the following Saturday.

A vastly-improved turnout of just over 35,000 pitched up at the Stadium of Light to get a taste of the new, improved Sunderland and pay homage to the new Messiah. Niall Quinn helped stoke up the fervour in his programme notes, describing Keane as 'a man who I am convinced is going to be one of the world's great managers.'

Leicester had themselves made a faltering start to the season, and all signs pointed towards a fourth straight win as the Royvolution gathered pace. Football doesn't work like that though, and the point gained from what ended as a 1-1 draw was most welcome. In a performance that harked back to the grim early days of the season, Sunderland were outfought, outworked and outplayed in the midfield from beginning to end.

Tobias Hysen, scoring his first goal for the club within minutes of coming on as a substitute, putting a 25-yard shot beyond the reach of the Foxes' 'keeper, salvaged a point, but the home side had set a benchmark at Derby and Leeds and for their next home match under Roy Keane, they let their standards slip. Every team has an occasional off-day, but when you're led by a character as exacting and demanding as Roy Keane, you don't get to do that too often and get away with it.

Daryl Murphy joined the lengthening queue of crocked forwards after a quarter of an hour, pulling up with a hamstring strain and giving Dwight Yorke 75 minutes to build up his match fitness, which in all honesty the veteran striker wasn't ready for. Yorke displayed some neat touches but looked well off the pace and it would take some time for him to acclimatise to the English game following his year in the Sydney paradise.

Keane described the disappointing result as 'a good reality check for everyone at the football club, especially the players.' The manager also revealed that he was quietly and diligently assessing his squad members and their response to being left out of the side. Hysen scored after being left out of the first two games and Keane said, 'I'm learning about the players every single day, and he hasn't come knocking on my door – like one or two others.'

Through its various incarnations in recent years, the second tier of the English game has proved to be far more intriguing than the 'best versus the rest' of the Premiership. The Championship is filled with teams who are all capable of beating each other on any given day – the teams who start the season badly rarely go down and the sides that fly out of the blocks often end up scrapping to hang on to a play-off place come the following Spring. Keane's arrival, the influx of so many new players and Sunderland's four-match unbeaten run had given the club's followers ample reason to believe that there was enough in the tank to have a good go at making one of the play-off places by the end of the season.

A week later, at Ipswich, and the opposite seemed the case. A 3-1 defeat and it looked as though Sunderland could be getting sucked back into a relegation battle. By the time it was all over, the Black Cats had deserved nothing from the match and Keane knew it. He'd spent most of the 90 minutes on the touchline, barking orders at his troops until he was hoarse.

Sunderland had taken the lead on the half hour when

Ipswich defender Jason De Vos turned the ball past his own goalkeeper after Ross Wallace had sent in a free-kick from the left-hand side. Parity was quickly restored by Darren Currie and Sunderland went in level at half-time but, as against Leicester, without playing to the maximum of their potential. Keane switched the team to a 4-5-1 formation at half-time, withdrawing Chris Brown, more out of necessity than anything else.

Brown had already been booked and would probably have gone on to pick up a second yellow card in what was a tetchy and niggly game. With no fit strikers available as substitutes, Dwight Yorke was forced to play up front alone for the second half, but his lack of pace and mobility meant that Sunderland were a busted flush in attack after half-time and two goals in three minutes from Ipswich's Alan Lee comfortably secured the points for the Tractor Boys. Ross Wallace added to the misery when he picked up his second booking in the 86th minute.

The unbeaten run and Keane's honeymoon period were at an end thanks mostly to some abominable defending and goalkeeping. The defeat clearly upset Keane but he was quick to declare afterwards that it didn't surprise him, saying, 'The staff, myself and the players know there's a lot of hard work ahead. We never thought we were the finished article, far from it.'

If they hadn't realised it already, the fans were starting to believe that the new manager had feet of clay and rocketing the team up the league table wasn't going to be on the agenda.

Meanwhile, fans who had invested in the club's shares in the past and still hoped to be able to hold on to them had their hopes finally dashed when Drumaville reached their target of 90% of the club's shares. This gave the consortium the automatic right to make a compulsory purchase of any remaining shares and take complete control of the club.

The next target to aim for was another three points from a visit to the Stadium of Light by Sheffield Wednesday. The match would be Sunderland's fifth in a busy three-week spell, and the last before a two-week break for international fixtures. The players had been itching to get at Sheffield Wednesday, eager to make up for the previous week's lacklustre effort at Portman Road. Keane made changes – Danny Collins was given a start at left-back while Tobias Hysen replaced the suspended Ross Wallace. Daryl Murphy had recovered from a hamstring injury and partnered Dwight Yorke in attack.

Although the final score was just 1-0, Sunderland were by far the better side with a whole host of players performing above their previous level. Ben Alnwick responded to criticism of his display at Ipswich with some match-winning saves while Stan Varga was impervious in the middle of the defence. Sunderland outplayed the visitors in every area of the field and the only negative was the lack of further goals that would have made the victory look as resounding on paper as it was on grass.

The winner was scored by Grant Leadbitter – a debut goal for a lad who had grown up supporting the club, and a player who Keane seemed to have been impressed by. Leadbitter's goal came just before the hour, Liam Lawrence whipping in a cross from the left and the young midfielder timing his run into the box perfectly, meeting the ball first time and sweeping it into the net from 12 yards out.

It would be a further fortnight before Sunderland's next fixture and so with just five players called up for international duty, it was almost a full-strength squad who headed off to the Algarve with Keane and his staff for a mid-season break. The Portuguese trip served a multitude of purposes. As well as a chance to take in some sun and train in more favourable conditions, Keane took the chance to observe his players at closer quarters and away from the regular day-to-day surroundings. He wanted to suss out those who were committed to themselves as footballers and those who were just along for the ride, the 'bluffers' as he had called them in the past. Those who didn't impress the new manager in the sunshine would almost certainly be heading elsewhere by the time the January transfer window opened.

CHAPTER FOUR

A DECADE OF LIGHT
MOVING IN AND MOVING UP

AS THEY PREPARED to enter the Premier League in August 2007, Sunderland AFC celebrated ten full seasons spent at their new home, the Stadium of Light. Although the ground is beginning to feel lived in and show signs of slight wear and tear, it is still a phenomenal stadium, and fans who pay a visit every other week can be forgiven for taking it for granted.

The short mile-and-a-half move from Roker Park to the Stadium of Light was a tortuous, drawn-out saga. For almost two decades before leaving the old ground, it was becoming obvious its days were over. As newer, tougher safety regulations were brought in by a government which seemed to regard football and its supporters as a blight on society, the capacity was slowly whittled away, the shrinking of the ground coinciding with a downturn in the club's fortunes. In particular the vast Roker End went from being a precipitous, imposing mass of swaying bodies to a scythed-down shadow of its former self.

Even in its final years, the old ground still managed to

play host to some memorable moments – the sight of Paul Hardyman following up a penalty which had been saved by Newcastle's John Burridge, by almost kicking the 'keeper's head clean off his shoulders will remain long in the hearts and minds of those who saw it. Then there was the penultimate league goal at the ground, a 20-yard free-kick hammered into the Fulwell End net by short-term player and lifelong fan Chris Waddle – his only goal for the club.

There were aspects of Roker Park that would disappear forever, not to be mourned, but which would grow fonder in memory as the years passed by. The electronic scoreboard that rarely worked, the tiny ticket office under the Main Stand, the ability of fans to climb up the floodlights for a better view. All of that and more was wiped clean away when the Stadium of Light opened for business in July 1997.

The bright, shiny new ground was playing host to a team that had just been relegated from the Carling Premiership a few months earlier. Managers at struggling top flight clubs always aim for the golden total of 40 points, safe in the belief that this will be enough to ensure survival. In 1996–97, Peter Reid's Sunderland got those 40 points but still went down, on the final day of the season at Wimbledon, with a vast army of travelling fans there to witness the sad finale. The team's problem had been its inability to score goals, the season's top scorers being Craig Russell and Paul Stewart with a risible four apiece.

One wonders how Sunderland would have fared without the long-term injuries to goalkeeper Tony Coton and striker Niall Quinn that blighted the season. Would those two have helped the side to the extra couple of points that would have ensured safety? Almost certainly.

With the new stadium came a new-look kit, club badge, nickname (the Rokerites had become the Black Cats) and a new-look team. The biggest signing was also the hardest to swallow – Lee Clark, from Newcastle United for £2.5 million. Way back in the past, players moving between the two rivals was a regular occurrence, but as the rivalry had turned to hatred over the previous decade, such transfers happened less and less. Clark would have a lot of work to do to win over cynical fans, who were also less than impressed with Reid's capture of a young Watford striker named Kevin Phillips.

Kevin who? Playing in a division below, Phillips had scored just four times in 16 matches in the season before the move, with three of those coming in the same game. A proposed move to Ipswich had just fallen through after the East Anglian club refused to stump up an extra £50,000 and the player ended up at Sunderland. The goal drought of the Premiership campaign didn't look like ending soon, despite the return to fitness of Niall Quinn, and other bargain basement signings, Chris Makin and Jody Craddock, had fans scratching their heads and opining that the Stadium of Light would be a complete waste of space without a competitive team playing in it.

Fears were allayed slightly on a gloriously warm Friday night in August 1997 when Quinn scored the first goal at the stadium, fittingly against Manchester City, his former club, in a 3-1 win. After City equalised the game was heading for a 1-1 draw, but the Phillips lad got a goal in the 84th minute and Lee Clark started to win over the sceptical fans with a third. But the state of the art Stadium of Light wasn't going to be a stage on which Sunderland could rip their way through the division without breaking sweat and instantly reclaim their place in the top flight.

Some indifferent form, including a 3-1 defeat at Port Vale and a 4-0 reverse at Reading, left the side shambling around in the bottom half of the table. With the fans' goodwill rapidly running out, Reid performed a cull after the defeat at Reading, drastically altering his defence.

Things started to improve with two wins and four draws in the next six league games, but then Peter Reid pulled his masterstroke on November 14th by doing a piece of business that should never be underestimated by Sunderland supporters.

Off to Manchester City went terrace hero and local boy Craig Russell and in his place came right-winger Nicky Summerbee. The deal was hugely unpopular with fans, saddened that one of their own had been shown the door, although in truth Russell's scoring record was never that great and what he lacked in composure and ball retention he more than made up for with pace, which never fails to excite fans and can win matches if deployed correctly.

So as the quick, popular Russell left, in came the languid, shabby-looking Summerbee, deemed a failure at Maine Road and with a lot of work to do to get in the good books of the Sunderland faithful. Scoring in his first appearance, after coming on as a substitute in a 4-1 win at Portsmouth, didn't do him any harm, although his ponderous approach to the game seemed an insult to fans who were mourning the loss of their hero. However, after Summerbee nailed down a starting place in the next game at Bury, the Black Cats won eight and drew two of the next ten matches, with Summerbee becoming the final piece in the jigsaw.

By now, Niall Quinn and Kevin Phillips had fully developed their striking partnership, with a healthy supply of crosses coming in from both flanks.

Summerbee played on the same right flank as his father, Mike, who won the league title with Manchester City and played eight times for England, while on the left, the duo of winger Allan Johnston and full-back Michael Gray were developing a special partnership. Johnston was a right-footed player, and was invariably shown inside by defenders whenever he made a charge down the wing.

The secret weapon however was Gray. Once Johnston started to go inside, Gray would bomb forward and offer support, giving Johnston the option of taking the ball inside with him or laying it out for Gray whose overlapping run could then continue on to the bye-line. The trick bamboozled teams week after week, with defenders confused and outnumbered, and tracking midfielders left in Gray's wake as he raced up the line to combine with Johnston and looked to get crosses in towards the front two.

Up front, Quinn and Phillips had become the epitome of the 'little and large' striking partnership. Despite his height and build, Quinn had a deceptively deft touch and was as comfortable with the ball at his feet as he was with it on his head. Likewise, for a small player, Phillips was no slouch in the air and was never afraid to try and win an aerial ball against a six foot plus centre half.

The centre of midfield was home to the industrious and skilful pairing of Lee Clark and Alex Rae, with Kevin Ball sporadically appearing as the season went on and players were rotated. Defensively, following the collapse at Reading, Reid put together a new-look youthful defence, with Darren Holloway making the right-back position his own and Jody Craddock and Darren Williams combining brilliantly as centre-halves. Williams and Holloway would celebrate call-ups to the England under-21 squad before the end of the season.

With a settled, winning system in place, the task was set for Sunderland to pursue the teams they'd allowed to open up a lead at the top of the table. At one point, Nottingham Forest and Middlesbrough had put 15 points between themselves and the Wearsiders, a gap that looked impossible to close as the two other sides jousted with each other for the table's top spot. But Sunderland had them in their sights and after the trip to Reading, the Black Cats lost just three matches in a 34-game run, championship form if it hadn't been for their miserable start to the season. Indeed, by way of a 4-1 win at Stockport in early March, Sunderland had amazingly barged their way into an automatic promotion place and it seemed certain that they would maintain their dizzying run of form and achieve the impossible dream in the first season at their new home.

Somehow, towards the end of that run, they drew two games in the space of a few days which they really should have won. On Good Friday, a 2-2 draw with QPR in freezing weather was a setback, particularly after the team was cruising with a 2-0 lead. The following Bank Holiday Monday, a 3-3 draw at West Bromwich Albion didn't help matters. Astonishingly though, Sunderland were still in second place and remained masters of their own destiny. They maintained their position with wins over Crewe and Stoke, but everyone at the top was winning at the same time and the sides could hardly be separated.

Losing the next game 2-0 at Ipswich all but condemned the Black Cats to the tension of the play-offs and after a last-day win at Swindon, it was confirmed that they had missed out on automatic promotion. So when Sunderland went to Bramall Lane for the first leg of the play-off semi-final against Sheffield United they had to get over the disappointment of finishing third and raise their game yet again. It was the fixture that had started the season back in August – Sunderland lost 2-1 that day and it was the same scoreline exactly nine months later. Kevin Ball's away goal gave Sunderland a lifeline to cling to but the return leg at Wearmouth would be all-or-nothing.

That match in the second leg of the play-off semi-final is repeatedly referred to by many of those who were there as the greatest they have seen in the decade the club have spent at the Stadium of Light. The ground was packed with 40,092 providing the kind of atmosphere no one knew would be possible in the new ground. It harked back to the glory nights at old Roker Park as the fans willed the players on to muster that extra effort and send them to Wembley.

The fans truly were the twelfth man on the pitch that evening, and an own goal from Nicky Marker followed by a Kevin Phillips strike gave Sunderland the two-goal cushion they needed before half-time. With nothing to lose, Sheffield United threw everything they had at Sunderland, pushing players forward in an attempt to level the aggregate score with a single goal. Lionel Perez was inspirational for Sunderland that night and when he made a double save at one point in the second half, it meant the Black Cats had done enough to go forward to Wembley and a one-off shot at promotion.

Kevin Phillips had enjoyed a phenomenal first season at the club, and doubts over the wisdom of signing him were quickly forgotten – his goal in the play-off semi-final was his 34th for Sunderland, equalling Brian Clough's post-war record for goals in a single season for the club. Wembley would give Super Kev the chance to make the record his own.

The match, against Charlton Athletic, stands the test of time as one of the greatest games ever played at the national stadium, particularly if you were a neutral. It wasn't one for admirers of the art of defending, as the two teams shared eight goals across 120 minutes of pulsating football. Phillips did get his 35th goal, chipping Sasa Ilic from distance, but his involvement would end soon afterwards when he picked up an injury and was withdrawn. Sunderland fans would be thwarted by one of their own, Clive Mendonca, born and bred in the city and scorer of a hat-trick for Charlton, as the goals kept flying in during a match which bordered on the surreal.

After extra time, and with the teams tied at 4-4, penalties would decide who would make it into the Premiership and collect the £10 million pound jackpot that came with a place in the top flight. In keeping with the attacking nature of the open play, both teams scored from their first six penalties. Then up stepped Michael Gray, the only other Sunderland-born player on the pitch. Preceded by a short run-up, his spot-kick was weak and Ilic made an easy save.

It was over. The season that heralded a new era at the club had started so frustratingly but Peter Reid had fashioned a side that was one of the most thrilling and attack-minded in the club's history. One season your top scorer gets four goals, the next season its 35! But Sunderland had faltered right at the last, in one of the most scintillating and heart-breaking games Wembley had ever seen. One team had a hero – Mendonca. The other team had a villain – Mickey Gray. They'd both gone to the same school – Castle View in Sunderland. Funny old game isn't it?

The Sunderland players weren't going to be damaged by the blow of losing at Wembley. They knew they'd been the best team in that league for the last three quarters of its season. All they had to do now was regroup, refocus and carry on exactly where they'd left off, with the lottery of a penalty shoot-out a distant nightmare.

Further strength had been added to the squad towards the end of the maiden season at the Stadium of Light with Danny Dichio arriving from Sampdoria, to primarily act as a stand-in should Niall Quinn be injured or exhausted. In the summer following Wembley, Reid again showed that he'd developed an eye for a bargain, bringing Denmark's second-choice goalkeeper Thomas Sorensen to the club for just half a million pounds.

A further million was paid to Bury for the services of Paul Butler, a strong, no-nonsense centre half. Reid's thinking was that if the goal scoring end of the team seemed to be taking care of itself, then a little extra security at the back would see them over the finish line in one of the top two spots in the division.

Any fears that there might be a hangover from the trauma of the previous season's finale were dismissed pretty quickly as Sunderland started the season with a blistering 24 game unbeaten run. Their motivation for the season didn't seem to be getting promoted, but rather getting promoted as quickly as was humanly possible.

But it wasn't without incident and worry. Lee Clark broke his leg on the opening day against QPR, leading him to miss the first three months of the season. In attack, Danny Dichio was quickly given a regular place instead of the injured Quinn and enjoyed a fan-pleasing run of five goals in four games.

Kevin Phillips didn't seem to mind playing with a different striking partner and simply carried on from where he'd left off with ten goals in the first eight games. He then picked up a minor toe injury, which became a major toe injury, eventually ruling him out for four long months.

The added strength at the back was paying dividends too, with new goalkeeper Sorensen a dramatic improvement on the hysterical, flapping hairball that was Lionel Perez. The Frenchman was a good shot-stopper, if somewhat prone to stopping them with his legs rather than his hands, but from a positional point of view he could be woeful, and was squarely to blame for Charlton's fourth goal at Wembley, when he jumped out to meet a cross he had no realistic hope of getting.

In September, four days after Kevin Phillips picked up his injury, Sunderland brought in Michael Bridges and it was Bridges and Dichio who got two goals apiece as Oxford were annihilated 7-0 at the Stadium of Light. Alex Rae came off the bench and also scored a couple and the goal tally could have been even higher as Dichio and Bridges both had goals disallowed.

Another notable victory came at West Bromwich Albion in October, where Sunderland shipped two goals in the first half and it looked as though they were heading towards the season's first defeat. The game changed completely when Michael Bridges came on as a second-half substitute, his pace tearing apart West Brom's defence which led to three goals and three more points for Reid's rampaging side.

The team were mean at the back and full of goals, in spite of the absence of Kevin Phillips, but the unbeaten run couldn't last forever and it ended at the Stadium of Light on November 21st where Barnsley won 3-2. By now, Sunderland were well clear at the top and already had one eye on promotion. The next test was to see how they could bounce back from defeat. It was a test they passed easily while managing to end the playing career of one of the country's best defenders from the previous decade into the bargain! A trip to Bramall Lane saw a resounding 4-0 win for the Wearsiders with two goals each for Niall Quinn and Michael Bridges. United's player-manager, and bent-faced Geordie, Steve Bruce had been so traumatised by Bridges' pace throughout the game that he promptly announced he would be hanging up his boots for good.

The Black Cats run of success continued with hardly a break, and they lost just once in the 11 league games following the Barnsley defeat, before facing Leicester City in the semi-final of the Worthington Cup. Kevin Phillips returned from injury for the trip to Queens Park Rangers in January – he could have been eased back into action from the bench, but he started the match and scored in a 2-2 draw. It felt as if he had never been away.

Now two legs against the Premiership's Leicester stood between them and a quick return to Wembley. But it wasn't to be, and Sunderland lost 3-2 on aggregate, the damage being done in a 2-1 defeat at the Stadium of Light for the first leg.

Although it was a disappointment, the focus remained on getting out of the First Division (as it was then) and into the big time again, to give the people of Sunderland the level of football their stadium deserved. There was a third defeat that campaign, at Watford, but it was to be the final blip as the Black Cats went on another astonishing unbeaten run which lasted for the remainder of the remarkable season.

The league-winning campaign of 1998–99 didn't have the roller-coaster factor of the previous year and as such it doesn't seem to have been remembered as fondly by fans as 1997–98 and Wembley and all that. But this record-breaking season still had its share of memorable games, one of the most bizarre being the trip to Bradford City. Naturally, Sunderland won, 1-0 on this occasion, but the scorer, Niall Quinn ended up keeping them out at the other end when Thomas Sorensen was stretchered off. As back then there were only three substitutes permitted, Sunderland didn't have a spare 'keeper, and so Quinn donned the special gloves and duly kept a clean sheet.

With Premiership football looming ever nearer, the ruthlessness with which Sunderland broke clear of the rest of the league was chilling, with 13 of the last 15 league games ending with yet another three points. Promotion was confirmed at Bury with a 5-2 win, including four goals from Phillips, and although he'd missed a large chunk of the season, Super Kev still scored 23 goals in 26 league games.

The league title was wrapped up three days later at Barnsley, 3-1 this time, and with three games to spare. The chase was now on to capture the record of most points in a league season. The record stood at 102, and Sunderland smashed it with 105, winning 31 out of their 46 league games. With an average crowd of over 38,000 for the season, the Black Cats had also the third-best attendances in England.

Plaudits rained down on the whole squad and Kevin Phillips and Michael Gray both celebrated call-ups to the England team, debuting against Hungary, a rare England appearance for players outside of the top flight. The squad was full of international players, all gearing themselves up for a crack at the big time. A lot had changed in the two seasons since the Roker Park side were relegated with low-scoring strikers. But although Sunderland AFC had the facilities, hard questions remained over whether the side could make the step up to the Premiership and make the grade on the pitch.

CHAPTER FIVE

POST-HOLIDAY HANGOVER

AS FAR AS the day-to-day running of football clubs goes, the season's sporadic breaks for international matches are a colossal pain in the backside. In addition to spending a fortnight fretting over the fitness of players who are away representing their countries, teams who are in a rich vein of form can find their good run abruptly put on hold and their momentum is often lost. Meanwhile, those teams in a slump have an aching length of time to brood over the whys and wherefores of their plight, without the chance to actually get out on the pitch and put it right.

In truth, as the start of October rolled around, Sunderland didn't fit into either of these categories. The win over Sheffield Wednesday meant that 13 points had been won from the six matches with Roy Keane in charge and the side were gradually beginning to creep up the table, sitting just five points shy of an automatic promotion spot. But two of the previous three games had ended in defeat and the faltering form needed to be addressed and dealt with. Cue an unhelpful 14 day break in between games.

Managers often use the international break to

allow players to slacken off a touch and recharge their batteries before reapplying themselves to the ongoing slog of the league campaign, hence Sunderland's trip to the Algarve.

The players continued to train as they soaked up the sun, concentrating on running and fitness work with some beach football thrown in. There was time for relaxation too, with some of the players taking in some golf along with a squad trip to a water park. Rumours that well-behaved players were rewarded with candy floss and a helium-filled balloon remain unconfirmed. Their return was delayed slightly – one holidaying fan witnessed the sight of Stephen Wright being asked to open up the plaster cast on his leg so that it could be checked. The right-back was not deemed a threat to European security and the squad returned to the north east.

Back on Wearside, and Keane's backroom staff was slowly taking shape. From Manchester United came Mike Clegg, their former full back, who had been working at the Old Trafford academy – he joined Sunderland as strength and conditioning coach. In addition came the offer of a permanent role at the Academy Of Light to Scott Ainsley, who took on a role combining the titles of fitness coach and sports scientist. Ainsley had worked with the club on a part-time basis since 1999 and his appointment increased the range of off-the-field resources available to Keane.

He would also soon subscribe to ProZone, a service which offers computerised analysis of every aspect of a match, adding yet another scientific dimension to his management arsenal. Clubs that use ProZone have fixed cameras around the ground that cover every single blade of grass, and almost as soon as a game has ended, managers can receive a detailed statistical breakdown of practically everything that happened during the 90 minutes.

Stats include basic info such as shots on and off target, as well as more detailed analysis; how much ground a player has covered during the match, breaking it down into sprinting, jogging and walking. Managers like Steve McClaren and Sam Allardyce were among the first to use ProZone and nowadays most of the top clubs have it, but at an average cost of £150,000 per year, it isn't cheap, and the idea of the club forking out for it during the final, financially-ruined years of the Bob Murray era would have been unthinkable.

Other business during the break saw two players heading out of the door, with Rory Delap leaving for Stoke City and Jon Stead going to Derby County, both on loan. The Delap deal included a permanent agreement to be completed in the January transfer window. For Stead, it gave him the chance of a fresh start as he sought to score the all-important goals that give arrogant, overpaid dimwits the right to be called professional footballers.

Ahead of the Preston trip, those five points separating Sunderland from a promotion place were making the disastrous start to the season look like more of an inconvenience than an obstacle. The Championship was settling down into its usual pattern of teams beating one another with a cluster of sides jockeying for position towards the top of the table. Preston North End were one of those in form, comfortably positioned in the top six, and with Keane identifying the trip to Deepdale as 'definitely the most difficult game we've had so far,' the match would prove to be a stern test of Sunderland's promotion credentials.

Again, the Black Cats were boosted by a huge away following, with 6,000 fans converging on the north west. Preston's bean-counters realised the financial boost they could receive from selling so many extra tickets and cleared out the whole of their Bill Shankly Stand for the day in order to accommodate the red and white army and maximise their income.

It is one of football's notorious unwritten laws that former players will come back to haunt you, and Sunderland fans should have been able to predict exactly what would happen when they realised that Danny Dichio would be lining up against them that afternoon. Dichio was never a popular player at the Stadium of Light, largely because if he was in the team it invariably meant that Niall Quinn wasn't, although the club have had far worse players acting as the 'big centre forward' both before and since, and the team benefited massively from the twelve goals Dichio scored in the 1998–99 promotion season.

If Sunderland fans were wary of Dichio's presence in the Preston line-up, further doom and gloom could confidently have been predicted when they realised that he hadn't scored a single league goal in the previous 18 months.

The script practically wrote itself and it was no surprise when Danny Dichio scored the opening goal in Preston's extremely comfortable 4-1 victory that day, the damage all done in a catastrophic first half for the Black Cats. Preston were easily the better side from the very start, playing a busy, fast-paced brand of football from the off, preventing Sunderland from playing and pressing them at every opportunity. It was under such pressure that those individual defensive errors that had almost become the Wearsiders' trademark all appeared again.

Graham Alexander had all the time and space he could possibly have needed to put a right-wing cross in after 18 minutes – the absence of any attempt at a clearance made it fairly simple for Dichio to nod the ball past Ben Alnwick and give the home side the lead. Preston doubled their advantage in the 31st minute after a wild lunging tackle from Nyron Nosworthy led to a penalty, which Alexander dispatched despite Alnwick's best efforts.

The game was over as a contest four minutes later when Preston striker David Nugent broke free in the final third, taking the ball wide of the 'keeper before crossing it straight into the path of the back-tracking Whitehead, who bagged himself an own goal as Preston piled on the misery.

Keane stood by the dugout, staring impassively across the carnage that had unfolded before his eyes. With the game over at 3-0 and the break approaching, it's likely that more than one of the Sunderland players were considering the appealing idea of skipping the dressing room altogether and just hailing a cab outside Deepdale while still in their kit, cutting their losses as far as football was concerned and making a fresh start in a new town. Maybe adopt a new identity... start again somewhere. Anything to avoid the roasting that would be coming to them behind the closed door of the dressing room during the interval.

Whatever was said or done at half-time had precious little effect. Sunderland refused to give up and gamely tried to chase a way back into the match, but the writing was on the wall when Nugent hit the bar five minutes after the restart quickly followed by a fourth Preston goal from Simon Whaley on 55 minutes, his long-range shot trundling past the hapless Alnwick. The 'keeper who Niall Quinn had compared to Roker legend Jimmy Montgomery at the start of the season was now beginning to look as capable between the posts as Jimmy Savile.

Minor consolation came when Stan Varga nodded home the first goal of his second Sunderland spell within a minute of Preston's fourth, rising above the home defenders to score, but the Black Cats fans had their tongues firmly planted in their cheeks when they set off on a conga around the Bill Shankly Stand towards the end of the match. A day out in nearby Blackpool would have been a much better bet.

Roy Keane had had enough. He'd played it cool in the face of defeat prior to Preston, but in the aftermath of the 4-1 result, he turned up the heat on his failing charges, saying, 'I think I've been relatively fair with my players... but I will be looking to get a more settled team from now on. The party is over for some of them.' The Irishman's assessment period had ended. Presumably some thought that, because they were getting games, their place in the comfort zone of the first team was assured. Not so – Keane had used the trip to the Algarve to judge his troops' attitude to their all-round duties as professional footballers while off the field, and maybe a couple of them had been selected for Preston in order to give them just enough rope to hang themselves.

'What I've seen recently has only confirmed what I might have thought about certain players when I first arrived seven weeks ago' said Keane. 'You get initial impressions when you first arrive but you've got to give people the benefit of the doubt but what I'm saying now just underlines what I thought then. I've now got to the stage where I know who I want to take with me and who I don't.'

Ben Alnwick, Liam Lawrence and Clive Clarke would be the casualties when the Sunderland's kamikaze away-day roadshow headed to Stoke, with five changes in all being made on the back of the Preston drubbing. Darren Ward got his first start as a Sunderland player in place of Alnwick, who, while being far from blameless, hadn't been helped by some idiotic defending in front of him. Perhaps the young 'keeper's time would come again. As for Clarke, he had never comfortably settled in at the Stadium of Light. After leaving Stoke in the summer of 2005 for West Ham when a move to Wearside had first been mooted, he'd made just three appearances for the Hammers and in the three games he'd played in the red and white, he looked like someone who was ill at ease with the professional game. To say that his fitness and desire looked questionable was to be polite. After a second half appearance at Stoke, Clarke's Sunderland career would fizzle out altogether.

To the Sunderland faithful, the third player to be dropped, Liam Lawrence, had become a love-hate figure. Some fans pointed to three brilliantly-taken goals in the Premiership as proof that 'Lenny' had the wherewithal to thrive at the highest level. Others reflected on his inability to get past defenders or provide threatening crosses as evidence in the case against. By the time of the Preston match, Lawrence was becoming the fans' boo-boy; expected to inspire at this level after a year in the Premiership, his career seemed to be hurtling backwards; struggling to hold down a place in the side, let alone complete 90 minutes when picked.

By speaking out after Preston and claiming that 'the party's over,' Roy Keane appeared to acknowledge the very definite end of a honeymoon period for him and his players, and some significant improvement was expected away at Stoke three days later. Helpfully, Stoke had ramped up the ticket prices for visiting Mackems after the sell-out trips to Derby and Ipswich, an increasingly regular practice around the country that was becoming known as the 'Magic Carpet Surcharge'. Sunderland fans vowed to boycott the Britannia Stadium catering in protest, although it is unknown how many unsold pies were handed out to dogs and tramps in the Stoke area afterwards.

Like Preston a few days earlier, Stoke's large, physical side went into the match looking to play at a high tempo and not let their opponents get a grip on the proceedings. It was a tactic which they employed successfully, but unlike at Preston, Sunderland rose to the challenge, and from the first kick the match was fiercely-fought, with players from both sides keen to indulge in the kind of old-school full-on tackling which fans love.

As part of his loan deal with Stoke, Sunderland had generously allowed Rory Delap to line-up for the Potters on the night, something which all parties would later end up regretting. The Irish utility player was just 11 minutes into his home debut for his new club when an innocuous challenge by Robbie Elliott left Delap with a broken leg and a premature end to his season. Stoke would later turn down the chance to cancel the permanent transfer of Delap, honouring the agreement they had with Sunderland and vowing to stick by the player during his recovery.

Either side could have taken the lead at the Britannia Stadium but it was Sunderland who went in front after 28 minutes when Dwight Yorke took advantage of some hapless flailing in the Stoke penalty area following a Liam Miller corner. The Stoke 'keeper (and Sunderland fan) Steve Simonsen got tangled up with his defenders, with the ball dropping for Yorke to hit home sweetly from ten yards.

The optimism generated by Yorke's goal evaporated with two Stoke goals in quick succession shortly after half-time. A high ball down the middle was almost bullied into the final third by Stoke's midfielders, Lee

Hendrie picking it up as it fell loose into space on the left-hand side and driving it past Darren Ward. Hendrie was on a long-term loan spell from Aston Villa where he had fallen out of favour, and his decade of Premiership experience shone through as he stamped his class all over the game, tormenting Nyron Nosworthy before leaving the field with ten minutes remaining, job more or less done.

As usual, Sunderland started to wobble following the equaliser and the winner duly came in the 54th minute, the Black Cats struggling to deal with a couple of deep crosses from both wings. The second one, from the left-hand side, was met with scarcely any resistance and Vincent Pericard stuck his free header away to put the Potters in the driving seat. Despite a couple of late chances that went begging, Sunderland never looked likely to get back into the match, their third consecutive defeat on the road.

For all the recent talk of being in touch with the promotion race, the Wearsiders had now taken just four points from five matches and a swing towards a relegation battle seemed just as likely. With seven defeats in the first twelve matches of the season and more than a quarter of the campaign gone, Sunderland were languishing in 19th place in the table.

Chairman Niall Quinn was obviously relatively happy with Keane's start however, as he chose to draw a line under his own brief managerial career, amusingly announcing his own retirement from club management, a decision which failed to rouse banner manufacturers or petition printers anywhere. Meanwhile, Keane's ongoing dissatisfaction with his defence led him to bring in Derby's Lewin Nyatanga on a three-month loan deal. Despite being capped by Wales when just 17, Nyatanga was struggling to hold down a place in the

Derby side, and a loan move was deemed to be the best move forward for both player and club.

With Barnsley sitting one place below Sunderland, the game on Wearside on October 21st had the makings of a drop-dodging six-pointer. The Yorkshire side were in the middle of a tailspin down the league and both sides required a win at all costs, with Keane urging his players to 'win ugly.'

As had become traditional, there were wholesale changes in the Sunderland line-up; perhaps Keane was picking his line-ups with a list, a blindfold and a dart. Kenny Cunningham returned in place of Robbie Elliott, while Lawrence, Brown and Murphy replaced Miller, Leadbitter and Wallace.

A disappointing crowd of just under 28,000 sat through an hour of another frustrating and unfulfilling Sunderland performance against a Barnsley side who seemed more than happy to soak up pressure and play for a point. Keane later reflected on the size of the crowd in relation to Sunderland's recent results and performances, stating, 'The attendance was a fair reflection on how we've been playing lately. It's like a movie – if you don't think it's any good, you won't go.'

The major plus for Black Cats supporters was seeing Dwight Yorke drop into a midfield role for the full 90 minutes. Yorke had played in the middle of the park for Trinidad and Tobago in the 2006 World Cup and was a revelation compared to the forlorn figure that had been seen turning out for Birmingham City a couple of seasons previously.

With more time on the ball and less pressure to expend energy looking for crucial positions in the final third, Yorke orchestrated most of Sunderland's play, and their inability to create any real chances stemmed from the absence of any supply from the wide men.

For one of your wingers to have a nightmare is unfortunate – for them both to turn in a stinker means you're in trouble, especially against a side who are happy to sit and let you come on to them. Against Barnsley, the performances of Liam Lawrence on the right and Daryl Murphy on the opposite side were wretched. Time and time again they were given the ball – usually by Yorke, although David Connolly's impressive hold-up play was also a positive factor, but the wide men produced nothing of any worth. Connolly did manage to beat the 'keeper early in the second half, but an offside flag only served to increase the mounting pressure throughout the stadium.

Eventually Murphy was hauled off and replaced by Ross Wallace, and as he sloped towards the touchline with his head bowed, it wouldn't have surprised anyone if the Irishman never pulled on a Sunderland shirt again. The introduction of Wallace followed a second-half debut for Lewin Nyatanga at left-back, and the pair combined well, with Nyatanga repeatedly keen to pick out a forward pass and Wallace unafraid to take on the defending full-back and create chances.

With the clock ticking, Sunderland's dogged determination finally bore fruit, but the opening goal actually came from the right-hand side, Nyron Nosworthy moving through the gears down the wing in the 82nd minute and sending a low ball into the box which Dean Whitehead managed to divert past the Barnsley 'keeper. It's a cliché, but the whole stadium did breathe a huge sigh of relief.

The breakthrough invigorated the Black Cats and their fans while demoralising the visitors, and a second goal came six minutes later. Ross Wallace twisted, turned and jinked his way past the full-back before crossing to the back post where Chris Brown was waiting to head the ball down and into the net, sealing the win for Sunderland.

The three points were more than welcome, and a quick look at the fixture list showed an intriguing couple of matches ahead – away at bottom-placed Hull followed by a home game against league leaders Cardiff. Two games that could very well bring out the best and worst of Roy Keane's Sunderland, although it would be impossible to predict which would be which.

CHAPTER SIX

KEEP THE FAITH

AS SUNDERLAND WERE scraping their way to a 2-0 win over Barnsley, Roy Keane had remained calm on the touchline, and the manager was equally philosophical afterwards, seemingly untroubled by how it had taken his team so long to break down the opposition's defence and secure the points. 'You tend to get people questioning things and the panic sets in,' he said. 'You just have to keep going. Keep bloody going.'

One man who did keep bloody going following the Barnsley win was jinxed defender Clive Clarke, who was sent to Coventry for a month-long loan spell. A Niall Quinn signing, the defender had never got to grips with life at the Stadium of Light, appearing in just four games, all of which had ended in defeat.

For the rest of the squad, one of the shorter trips of the season, to Hull City, followed, with a strong chance to chalk up a second consecutive win – the fact that Hull were sitting at the bottom of the table couldn't hurt.

During his infamous 'prawn sandwich' rant in 2000, Roy Keane was quick to identify a section of the Manchester United home support as the focus of his anger, and he made the point of praising the club's travelling fans, saying, 'Away from home, the fans are fantastic; I'd call them the hardcore fans.' That same 'hardcore' term also applies to Sunderland's away support. At the Stadium of Light, supporters find it easier to barrack the players if the side aren't in front by half-time, while simultaneously failing to realise that a lot of visiting teams are content to play with men behind the ball, frustrating Sunderland while looking to exploit any counter-attacking opportunities that might arise. But those who go on the road to follow the team are a different breed altogether. Wins are celebrated more intensely and defeat tastes all that more bitter (see Southend and Bury in August 2006). To Hull, as ever, Sunderland took as many away fans as the opposition would allow, in excess of 4,000 on this occasion.

Following six games in the red and white and still without a goal to his name, David Connolly was dropped to the bench and a slow-moving 'Big & Bigger' striking duo of Chris Brown and Daryl Murphy started the match. Sunderland dominated the game throughout, landing nine shots on target and controlling the play in midfield. Dwight Yorke again showed his vision and composure in midfield, and it was now starting to become apparent why Keane had whisked his former team-mate halfway around the world to join the cause.

But there was still one missing ingredient – goals. If Barnsley was a late, late show, then Hull was a test of how far the fans could bite what remained of their fingernails. As the seconds ticked away, a draw looked the likely outcome, in spite of Sunderland's domination of possession. It was deep into injury time at the end of the second half when the winning goal finally arrived. Ross Wallace had drifted across to the right-hand side and picked up the ball; sensing space, he ghosted into Hull's penalty area and curled a shot wide of their 'keeper with what was practically the last kick of the match.

The red and white army behind the goal went berserk, with Wallace racing towards them, whipping off his shirt in celebration. Fans spilled out of the stand and mobbed the winger, but once order had been restored (and a large number of Hull fans had started heading home), the referee had no option but to show Wallace a yellow card for leaving the field of play. Unfortunately, as it was his second of the match, the yellow was swiftly followed by a red, but Wallace was undaunted and gave a clenched-fist victory salute to the away fans as he headed towards the tunnel.

So, with a handful of seconds remaining, the points were Sunderland's, and the win meant they moved up to a far healthier league position of 13th. Their newly-acquired ability to cover every last blade of grass and compete for every last second of the 90 minutes was starting to be converted into points won, an encouraging product of the new, improved Keane regime.

By rights, the back to back victories, coupled with the quality of the performance at Hull, should have given Sunderland sufficient momentum to take into their next match against league leaders Cardiff, and the players ought to have been brimming with confidence. In terms of team selection, Keane was still yet to field an unchanged side from one game to the next and certain areas were proving problematic.

The manager seemed no nearer to finding a right-back who he was happy with – against Cardiff it was the turn of Neill Collins, following Whitehead and Nosworthy in the previous two matches, with Whitehead reverting to midfield for the visit of the league leaders. The unwieldy pairing of Brown and Murphy were again selected to lumber around together up front, Connolly ruled out with a late hamstring injury. The treatment room had finally begun to quieten down too, with Steve Caldwell,

Stephen Elliott and Graham Kavanagh all returning from injury to start among the substitutes.

With hindsight, any Sunderland fan that backed his side to win on October 31st 2006 must have had a screw loose. Look at the ingredients for the visit from Cardiff that night. The Welsh side had stormed clear at the top of the league.

Their leading goal scorer was a former Newcastle United prodigy who had scored his one and only Premiership goal in the Wear/Tyne derby at the Stadium of Light the previous season. Plus, the whole thing was taking place on the night of Halloween. When an actual magpie appeared in the Stadium out from nowhere after Chopra gave Cardiff the lead, staying to hop about on and around the pitch for the rest of the game, there could be no doubt which side would come out on top that night.

The Black Cats weren't helped in the slightest by the reappearance of their ugliest traits; namely defensive sloppiness and a complete lack of creativity. To make it worse, the man voted Sunderland's Player of the 20th Century, 'King' Charlie Hurley, was the club's guest of honour for the evening; the legendary centre half would have been dismayed by the defensive incompetence that crippled the Wearsiders' chances.

Hurley was invited by Niall Quinn to attend the match and to see the Chairman's Suite at the Stadium of Light renamed as The Charlie Hurley Suite. Ahead of the match, Quinn paid tribute to the Corkman, explaining, 'Charlie still has such an influence on this club it's incredible. Most of my investors – the Drumaville consortium – are here because as younger men Charlie was a big part of their lives.'

Sunderland were behind in under four minutes, Stan Varga completely misjudging a deep cross and allowing

Michael Chopra all the time and space in the world to convert easily from six yards, a good three yards further out than the young forward had been when he scored for Newcastle at the Stadium of Light in April that year. After the less-than-hospitable reception he'd received from the home support, Chopra was only too keen to celebrate his goal in front of the home fans in the North Stand, something which served only to wind the fans up further.

To their credit, the Wearsiders didn't take long to level things up, Chris Brown heading forcefully past Neil Alexander from Hysen's well-placed left wing cross. But it was a false dawn, with too many Sunderland players lacking the ability to compete against a side who had earned their place at the top of the table and who were playing with appropriate pomp and swagger. It was a bad, bad night for Stan Varga, who was caught daydreaming again for what would be Cardiff's winner, eight minutes before half-time.

As with the first goal, a ball came in from the right which appeared to confuse the Slovakian defender – his positioning was marginally better this time but he seemed to try and spin and hook the ball away in the direction in which it was travelling. Enter Michael Chopra again, who instinctively poked it into the back of the net. Cue another arrogant celebration, and further noise and fury from the North Stand.

Shortly afterwards, as if to rub salt into the wound, the magpie appeared and proceeded to hop around for the remainder of the match, infuriating some of the more 'sensitive' Sunderland fans. Perhaps Chopra had been concealing it in his shorts, as a gesture from one Geordie to over 25,000 Mackems. Think you've seen everything at a football match? This author witnessed a grown man being held back by two of his friends as he attempted to get on to the pitch, presumably with the intention of maiming the bird that represented everything he hated. You don't get that sort of thing at the snooker.

Afterwards, Keane was the model of suppressed rage, refusing to answer press questions with sentences that were any longer than three or four words, repeatedly using the word 'poor.' The feeling was that if he started to elaborate and express his heartfelt opinion, the gentlemen of the press would bear witness to the first outburst that so many of them had thought would become a regular part of the Roy Keane rollercoaster football manager experience.

Stopping short of verbally tearing a strip off his players, Keane hinted at what he felt the fundamental problem was throughout the team – a lack of ruthlessness. He said, 'The players need to get a hold of each other sometimes, there's no need to be such pals with each other. I played with lads I never spoke to for years but I was still glad they were on my team.'

After the match Keane was introduced to his fellow Corkman for the first time, and later said, 'I met Charlie Hurley after the game, a top player at this club and he spoke more sense than anyone I've met in a long, long time'. The respect was clearly mutual, and despite the evening's result and performance, the King of Sunderland was quick to praise the new regime at the club. Hurley said, 'Roy and Niall are leaders and they know what's needed. Roy was not a happy man after the game because he is a winner. I told him he has a lot of work to do and he understands that.'

Despite the disappointment of the Cardiff result, the inconsistent nature of the Championship meant that Sunderland were still only six points adrift of a play-off spot and with more than six months of the season to play, there was still plenty of time for them to get in among the shake-up and maybe be involved in the end-of-season knockout competition.

Neill Collins had been one of the worst players on the pitch against Cardiff and a few days later he was on his way to Wolves on a loan deal, where he would once again link up with Mick McCarthy, the manager who had brought him to Wearside from Dumbarton. This followed the revelation from Keane that there had been communication between himself and Mick McCarthy, presumably for the first time since Keane stormed out of the Republic of Ireland camp ahead of the 2002 World Cup.

As managers in the same division, it was always a case of when, rather than if the pair would come face to face and Sky Sports had opted to screen the upcoming Molineux clash between Wolves and Sunderland so that they could broadcast the historic moment to a salivating nation. A few days before Collins was shipped out to the Midlands, Keane had revealed that, 'Mick rang up about one of our players. We had a chat, that's it.' Evidently, that player was Neill Collins. As with Rory Delap, the loan deal would be become permanent in the January 2007 transfer window.

Next up was an away day at Norwich City, by no means an easy fixture on paper, but one which Sunderland had to get something from if their new-found credibility was to remain intact. Not surprisingly, Stanislav Varga was dropped, with skipper Steve Caldwell returning after his long-term injury. Following the Neill Collins loan deal, it was Dean Whitehead's turn to play at right-back, with Graham Kavanagh returning to the side in midfield after injury.

David Connolly had overcome his hamstring injury and was restored to the starting line-up, Keane seemingly unconcerned by his striker's inability to get his first goal for the club.

Proving that they'd learned that it doesn't pay to upset Roy Keane two matches in a row, Sunderland's players put in a greatly improved performance following the debacle of the Cardiff match, yet astonishingly came away with nothing. Norwich scandalously took all three points with what was practically their sole chance in the match. Breaking away from a spell of Sunderland pressure and shifting the ball upfield, it was played into the path of Robert Earnshaw, one of the quickest forwards in the Championship. With Sunderland's defence breached, the Welsh international raced forward and swept a shot past Ward from the edge of the area, just after half-time.

The sense of injustice was only increased after Sunderland had two blatant penalty claims rejected by referee Mike Riley in the space of a couple of minutes, midway through the second half. Riley, an occasionally controversial referee, famously enraged the president of Levski Sofia after he had sent off one of his players in a UEFA Cup semi-final.

After that particular match, the furious president referred to Riley as a 'British homosexual,' but the ref was called far worse by Sunderland fans at Carrow Road that afternoon when he waved away the penalty claims. The first looked as blatant a foul as you'll ever see in the box, Daryl Murphy going down after being tackled from behind by Dion Dublin. A second shout, for what looked very much like a handball, also by Dublin, was again ignored by Riley, the type of referee who does nothing to remove the negative stereotyping that surrounds the game's whistle-blowers.

This was the team's ninth defeat in 16 league outings and the first time the side had failed to score since

Keane took over. The Irishman's debut season as a manager wasn't going to be a tale of instant glory or an immediate emulation of the success that he achieved as a player at Manchester United.

With two defeats in the space of a few days, Sunderland had started dropping down the league table again and were now in 17th position. Thoughts of the play-offs, let alone automatic promotion, were now looking very ambitious.

Niall Quinn wasn't alarmed by the team's stuttering form on the pitch, and reiterated his belief that Roy Keane was the right choice for the job during a Q&A session on the club's official website, telling fans, 'I am very, very comfortable knowing that everything Roy has epitomises what I want brought into this football club.'

The chairman outlined his relaxed approach to his own working relationship with Keane, adding, 'I am not up high looking down on the manager, saying, "You better do this, you better do that", as happens at a lot of football clubs.'

Quinn also told the club website of the resistance that the Drumaville consortium members faced from their financial advisors before launching the takeover bid. He said, 'Every one of the financial advisors to the eight of us in the Drumaville investment team were told not to do it. So that just gives fans an idea of what they have agreed to do, and that they all went against their financial advice.'

The chairman restated that the consortium would be aggressive in player recruitment as they aimed to take the club forward and try to reach the Premiership, adding, 'We've looked at all areas and we know this club needs to buy players. We've identified the kind of players that are required and we hope to compete above our weight, be the leading instigators, if you like, in player transfers in this division.'

These were words that were aimed at placating fans who were beginning to have doubts about the ambitions of the club's new owners. Results weren't going as well as all had hoped and questions were starting to be asked about Keane's ability to haul the side into the top flight. The cynics were still hovering, waiting for a row to break out between manager and chairman that would lead to Keane walking away from the job.

But Quinn believed wholeheartedly in his manager and was also looking to his own future, divulging that he already had a personal exit strategy in place. He had previously spoken of a five-year plan, but revealed more to safc.com, explaining, 'I would be happy when we have had three years of Premiership football. That for me would be the stability the club has lacked over the years.' Quinn explained that he would then look to walk away and hand over control to a suitable successor, saying, 'If, after that period of time, we have brought it to a level and we feel that the club has started to standardise itself as a Premiership club and somebody else wants to come in and try to kick on again, I will walk.'

But all talk of stability in the Premier League was very far-sighted when the team were unable to put together any kind of winning run in the Championship to avoid the season becoming a write-off. Their next chance came against Southampton at the Stadium of Light. Ahead of the game, Roy Keane pinpointed what he felt was the crucial flaw in his team at that time, saying, 'We've got a lot of players who are very comfortable in possession but what we need is players running off the ball, players creating space for others by making runs which stretch the opposition.'

Against Southampton, Sunderland showed more of the cleverness that Keane was striving for, but the afternoon would end in further misery. The paying public were not impressed by the way things were going either, and while 25,667 is far from a poor attendance, especially outside the Premier League, Quinn would have been dismayed that his magic carpet hadn't picked up a significant number of new passengers, the Stadium of Light looking under-populated with large patches of empty red seats providing a backdrop to the action.

The home fans approached the game hoping that their former 'keeper Kelvin Davis would turn in one of the performances that saw his stay on Wearside curtailed after the previous relegation season, but it was the home goalkeeper who stood out most on the day, Sunderland once more undone by an impotency in the final third of the pitch.

Despite all of their huffing and puffing, Sunderland actually took the lead just after the hour. For years the side had been bereft of anyone who could pose a threat from direct free-kicks.

Julio Arca had his moments, but Black Cats fans were becoming achingly familiar with the sight of a free-kick either failing to clear the defensive wall or go sailing up towards the fans behind the goal. But against Southampton, Ross Wallace hit the target in deadly fashion, lifting his free-kick up and around the wall and past Davis.

Having learnt from past experience, the winger restricted his celebrations to a knee slide towards the corner flag while keeping his shirt on.

Darren Ward later pulled off a wonder save from Pedro Pele. Keane said afterwards it was 'as good a save as I've seen.'

Some people compared it to the world class save by

England's Gordon Banks against Brazil in the 1970 World Cup – coincidentally that save was also from a header by Pele.

Southampton ratcheted up the pressure as the game entered its dying moments and although their equaliser was hard to swallow it was hardly a shock. Gareth Bale, their best player by far and a youngster surely bound for bigger and better things, hit a speculative drive from the edge of the area which took a cruel deflection from Steven Caldwell, robbing the Black Cats of three much-needed points, and sinking them to 19th in the table. The wicked deflection made it something of a freak goal, and it was likely to be the only way that Darren Ward would be beaten, such was the level of his performance.

So, two and a half months into Roy Keane's tenure as Sunderland manager, and since winning at Derby County, the team had climbed a mere two positions in the table. For all of his big talk and bigger changes, a relegation scrap was looming. A lot was wrong. Defensively, there was no selection consistency, which had a lot, but not all to do with injuries. The team had started each of the last five games with a different right-back to the one before, and Keane was still no closer to deciding what his preferred centre half pairing would be. In midfield, the impact and influence that Graham Kavanagh was supposed to bring had been blunted by his injury problems.

Another new recruit to the centre of midfield, Liam Miller, couldn't hold down a place in the team. Invention was in short supply, with the most gifted player at the club, Dwight Yorke, seemingly unable to get through a full 90 minutes each week, and playing in a deeper role than at any time in his career, expected to prompt the rest of the midfielders.

Players like Liam Lawrence, who the fans were starting to turn against and whose career now looked to be hurtling backwards.

David Connolly, who Keane had charged with scoring the goals to propel the team up the league, had so far failed to hit the back of the net in nine attempts. His hold-up play and movement were superb, and his barren run would certainly not last forever, but his striking colleagues were Stephen Elliott, who in truth had contributed very little in the way of goals since January 2005, and the workhorse duo of Chris Brown and Daryl Murphy, neither of whom looked like being the 15 goals a season man that Sunderland would surely need if they were to make any impact on the league.

It was a complete mystery as to which way the team would head next.

CHAPTER SEVEN

A DECADE OF LIGHT
PREMIER PASSION

AS IN 2007, the promoted Sunderland side of 1999 went into the season with the vast majority of their supporters fully behind the club and its aims. Under Roy Keane and with two weeks to go to the start of the season, the club reported that 30,000 season tickets had been sold. Back in 1999, the figure was 36,000. With the stadium capacity stuck at 42,000 in those days, this was an impressive number, meaning that every single home game would be practically a sellout. With the revenue generated from 1999's advance ticket sales, chairman Bob Murray and the board loosened the purse strings in order to let Peter Reid compete with other Premiership clubs.

Reid had adopted a cautious approach to player recruitment to date, striking lucky with bargains like Kevin Phillips, Thomas Sorensen, and Allan Johnston. Although the club were now operating at a higher level than they had for decades, he still wasn't prepared to needlessly squander millions on unproven players. Well, maybe just one – Carsten Fredgaard was an unknown Danish left-winger who could also play up front. Reid paid £1.7 million for Fredgaard, but the player made just one league appearance for the club, and that was as a substitute. Fredgaard gradually disappeared, almost without trace, and by 2007 was playing in the Danish second division for Randers FC at their 12,000 capacity Essex Park ground.

Reid spent much less money on far better players. Although both were firmly in the 'veterans' category, Steve Bould's services were acquired from Arsenal for £500,000 while German international Thomas Helmer arrived from Bayern Munich on a Bosman free transfer, both players brought in for their wisdom and professionalism as much as anything else. One thing was for certain, Helmer's 68 German caps and sackful of medals would look impressive around the place. The big purchase of the summer had been Stefan Schwarz, the Swedish international who, at the age of 30, had experience at the top level in Portugal, England, Italy and Spain and arrived from Valencia for £4 million.

With the new recruits added to the squad that had torn through the First Division, Sunderland looked to be in good shape as they prepared for the rigours of the Premiership. That was until Reid dropped a bombshell on the first day of pre-season training – he was ready to sell three of the key players who had won the league just months earlier.

Two of them, Allan Johnston and Michael Bridges, had refused to sign new contracts and with just twelve months remaining on their current deals, would both be entitled to leave for free at the end of the coming season. Today, with the Bosman ruling fully embedded into the European game, players who are truly wanted by their clubs are rarely allowed to enter the final year of their deal without an extension being negotiated and signed but then clubs were still feeling their way around the logistics of the new ruling.

It was suggested that the two players had verbally agreed terms with Reid on the end of season team getaway, but had reneged on this once they had arrived home. The manager announced they would be frozen out of all first team activity unless they agreed to the original terms of the proposed contract extensions.

Bridges soon moved on to Leeds United for £5 million and was an immediate hit in the Premiership, while Johnston sweated it out, training with the youths and biding his time before moving to Rangers in the summer of 2000. The Scottish international had used the Bosman ruling to his advantage once before, when he moved from Hearts to French side Rennes in 1996, and so it was no surprise that he was happy to take a year out of his career in order to get the move to the club he supported as a boy.

The third player to be transfer-listed on that day of the long knives was Lee Clark. Pictures had appeared in the press of Clark enjoying a day out at the FA Cup final, watching his beloved Newcastle be comfortably outplayed by Manchester United. Nothing wrong with that, apart from the fact that Clark was pictured wearing a T-shirt emblazoned with the slogan 'Sad Mackem Bastards.' Oh dear.

Footballers have a reputation for not always being the crunchiest biscuits in the tin, and their lack of intelligence can be excused up to a point, as when most kids were paying attention at school, future footballers were dreaming about being out on a field, playing football. But what Clark did was so bone-headedly pig-ignorant that it defies belief. He later said that he'd been unable to envisage playing for Sunderland against Newcastle, something which he would have had to do in a matter of weeks, so it was probably in everyone's best interests that he left the club if he couldn't commit himself fully to the cause.

But Clark had been outstanding in his two seasons on Wearside and was a major influence on the success the team had at that time. Along with Bridges and Johnston, he would be a major miss. He was swiftly moved on to Fulham for a fee of £3 million, giving Sunderland a slight profit on their original outlay.

The popular reaction to Reid's actions was stunned disbelief. Few could believe that a manager would hamper his side's chances in what was already set to be a relegation battle by surgically removing such an important chunk of his team before a ball had even been kicked. Pundits had a field day, including Sky Sports' Rodney Marsh, who predicted instant relegation for Sunderland and claimed that Kevin Phillips would struggle to score more than six goals all season.

A 4-0 defeat at Chelsea on the opening day of the season suggested the likes of Marsh and his colleagues might be right. Behind the scenes, further unrest was reported. Thomas Helmer had failed to nail down a place in the starting line-up, making just one full appearance in the first few games, and rumours of a backroom bust-up between the German and Bobby Saxton quickly spread.

Sunderland later intimated that Helmer did not meet the fitness criteria they had required and he was quietly dispatched back to Germany, where he enjoyed a fruitful Champions League campaign with Hertha Berlin.

After four games, Sunderland had four points on the board, which wasn't fantastic but wasn't a disaster either. But four points was three more than their neighbours at Newcastle United had managed to acquire, and serious pressure was being applied to the Magpies' manager Ruud Gullit as the Wear–Tyne derby loomed, particularly as tension had been reported between Gullit and Geordie pin-up Alan Shearer.

The short trip to St James' Park was made on a Wednesday evening in what could modestly be described as a monsoon. With the enemy seemingly in turmoil, Sunderland fans sensed that victory could be theirs for the taking and hilarity ensued when the team line-ups were revealed. Presumably in order to show him who was boss, Shearer had been dropped to the bench by Gullit, along with Scottish international Duncan Ferguson. Instead, Newcastle would play with a lone striker, Paul Robinson, a former Darlington player who also happened to be a dyed-in-the-wool Sunderland supporter. Although not much of a footballer.

As the game commenced, thunder crashed through the night sky, and the torrential rain began to form puddles on the playing surface. Both sides attacked although Sunderland created the better chances in what quickly became an open contest, but an abandonment always looked a distinct possibility. Sunderland fans started praying for more rain when Newcastle took the lead through Kieron Dyer, who deftly lofted the ball over Sorensen after 28 minutes.

As the scoreline remained 1-0 into the second half, the quality of football deteriorated further. The puddles on the pitch were turning into small lakes and players were aquaplaning across the surface as they threw themselves into tackles. The ball was holding up in the water more and more and both sides began to resort to a game of lump and chase. Paul Robinson was withdrawn by Ruud Gullit, but his replacement was Duncan Ferguson, further humiliating Alan Shearer.

Sunderland's equaliser came on 64 minutes. A right-sided free-kick by Nicky Summerbee reached Quinn at the near post. He held off his defender and flicked a header past Tommy Wright in the Newcastle goal. The tide was turning and it was beginning to look as though the script might have been written for Sunderland. The clamour for the introduction of Alan Shearer became overwhelming and he was finally introduced into the match as a response to Quinn's goal.

But within minutes, Sunderland were ahead. Summerbee was again the architect, launching a long cross to the far post where Kevin Phillips was in oceans (almost literally given the conditions) of space. His shot was poor, and it bounced straight back off Tommy Wright.

In normal conditions it would have rolled towards the touchline but instead it got held up in the sodden penalty area. Thinking on his feet, Phillips raced to retrieve it and sent a first-time looping shot back towards the Newcastle goal. It seemed to hang in the air as it sailed over Wright and a defender before dropping into the goal to give Sunderland the lead.

At the Stadium of Light, thousands of fans had converged to watch a live beam-back of the match on a giant screen erected on the pitch. Some fans also hired out executive boxes and enjoyed the entertainment with an unending supply of cold drinks. The atmosphere at the stadium was wilder than it would normally have been for an ordinary home match.

Newcastle's only real chance of an equaliser came in a suitably bizarre fashion when Duncan Ferguson and Kevin Ball went in for a challenge 35 yards from Sunderland's goal. The ball bounced off the Sunderland player and went flying back towards his own goal, evading Sorensen before thankfully bouncing off the top of the crossbar and going out for a corner.

The final whistle was met with jubilation by the 850 Sunderland fans who had been allowed into St James' Park, and, with a cacophony of booing from the enraged home supporters, Ruud Gullit's time on Tyneside was up. He resigned as manager three days later, blaming media intrusion into his private life. Nothing to do with being disgraced at home against your biggest rivals while you selected an untried boy over one of the country's most prolific strikers then?

The win at St James' kick-started Sunderland's season and heralded a run of seven wins and a draw in their next eight matches, including a 5-0 win at Derby and a 4-0 victory at Bradford City. Kevin Phillips and Niall Quinn had continued where they'd left off the season before, with Phillips scoring 13 times in Sunderland's first twelve matches while adding to his burgeoning collection of England caps.

On October 24th, the Black Cats travelled to West Ham sitting in second place in the table. Despite Steve Bould being sent off in under 20 minutes, Sunderland took the lead through Phillips and held on, almost until the bitter end. West Ham snuck an equaliser from Trevor Sinclair with two minutes to play and the Wearsiders had to settle for a draw. If they'd held on and won they would have been top of the table.

Sunderland were undaunted and the unbeaten run continued as Chelsea arrived on Wearside, chock full of international superstars and managed by the likeable and laid-back Gianluca Vialli. The Black Cats destroyed them in an astonishing first-half performance which saw half-time arrive with them leading 4-0. They didn't just score four goals, they scored four great goals, the pick of them being the last, a Phillips 30-yard screamer that almost lifted the roof off the stadium. With the job done, the second half was jaw-grindingly awful, like the worst kind of hangover, and Chelsea scored a late consolation. But the match confirmed that with the new home selling out every week, Sunderland were aiming for the stars, eager to seal a place at the top table of the game.

The Wearsiders only lost twice again before Boxing Day and stayed in the race for European qualification, something which would have been unimaginable back in July when Clark, Bridges and Johnston were transfer-listed. The squad was added to with the addition of Kevin

Kilbane from West Bromwich Albion for £2.2 million, although the left-winger would not enjoy a happy time on Wearside. He was not solely to blame, but the side's good run ended as soon as Kilbane started his first match in the red and white.

As Sunderland reached the magical 40-point survival figure just before Christmas, a 5-0 Boxing Day defeat at Everton signalled the start of an alarming tailspin and they wouldn't win again for another three months. In the middle of all of that came one of the strangest transfer stories at Sunderland or any other club in recent years. On deadline day in March 2000, the signing of Milton Nunez was announced for £1.6 million. A Honduran international striker, his nickname was Tyson, and great things were promised if Peter Reid was to be believed.

A few days later, at half-time during the home win over Everton, Nunez was introduced to the crowd. It was immediately apparent to all but the most short-sighted of fans that the man being paraded before them was far, far too small to be a professional footballer in one of the top leagues in the world. 'Tyson' looked less like a footballer and more like the character of Arnold from the 1970's American sitcom *Diff'rent Strokes* but fans were told that he would soon become their new hero.

Something went awry somewhere because Nunez played just 15 minutes of league football for Sunderland, as a substitute against Wimbledon. Like Carsten Fredgaard before him, big money had been squandered with no return whatsoever. Stories later emerged claiming that there was another Nunez who played for Honduras who Sunderland should have signed, but owing to some kind of communication breakdown, they ended up with this midget from the country's third division. It wouldn't be the last time Reid got his spending spectacularly wrong.

In the end, the 4-1 victory over Chelsea was almost

the story of Sunderland's season writ small – spectacular in the first half, dire in the second. After three winless months they got back into the groove, ironically in the return fixture with Everton, triumphing 2-1, as part of a run of five victories in their final nine matches, but it wasn't quite enough to seal a European place and the club finished in seventh. In truth, everyone connected with the club should have been delighted to have made such an impact on the Premiership at the first attempt, but the poor run of post-Christmas form and narrowly missing out on Europe left a sour taste.

The highlight of the campaign was the performances of Kevin Phillips. He ended the season with 30 goals in 36 league appearances, winning the Golden Boot of Europe, the only Englishman to pick up the coveted award for the top scorer in the continent. Phillips was a rare gem of a player, and linked up perfectly with Niall Quinn as probably the best striking partnership Sunderland fans had ever seen. The next test was to do it all again.

Players and fans were chomping at the bit for the 2000–01 season to get underway to see if they could repeat and improve on the club's performance on their inaugural Premiership season at the Stadium of Light. With bumper crowds comes bumper money, and Peter Reid's transfer kitty grew larger. In came Everton's Don Hutchison for £2.5 million, Argentine under 21 international Julio Arca for £3.5 million and a Slovakian centre half, Stanislav Varga, for just under a million.

Varga's debut against Arsenal on the first day of the 2000–01 can be added to the list of memorable Stadium of Light games. The defender had an absolute blinder, winning headers left, right and centre, reading the game to snuff out potential danger, timing tackles to perfection both inside and outside the box, and sending long, raking passes forward from the back, opening up the game and creating attacking options for Sunderland, in a match which they won 1-0. In Varga's second game, at Manchester City, he picked up a career-threatening injury which kept him out of the side for two months and he was never the same player again.

Again the side made a slow start to the season, losing three out of their first five matches before embarking on another strong run, with just two defeats in 21 league outings. The start of the run coincided with the arrival of Chelsea's Emerson Thome for a fee of £4.5 million, and the Brazilian added an element of steel to the back line.

The highlight of that string of impressive results was another visit to St James' Park and another 2-1 win. Once more, Sunderland made it hard for themselves by going behind to an early goal, but Niall Quinn got on the score sheet again, grabbing the winner this time after self-confessed Toon supporter Don Hutchison scored the equaliser and endeared himself to the Mackem fans by racing towards them and kissing the badge on his shirt. The feeling that these fixtures were being staged purely as a source of humiliation for Alan Shearer was strengthened when the Newcastle captain had a chance to equalise from the penalty spot 11 minutes before the end. With the help of some furious gesturing towards his left-hand side from Hutchison, Thomas Sorensen chose correctly and parried Shearer's penalty.

The results kept on going Sunderland's way, with a couple of 4-1 wins over the Christmas period, against Bradford and Ipswich, as well as a hard-fought 2-2 draw at Arsenal. As in the previous season, the trip to West Ham was again loaded with significance – a 2-0 win at Upton Park in January saw Sunderland climb back up to second place. They were competing for European football again, but the question was familiar – could they sustain their push or would they suffer a second consecutive collapse?

It was the latter, and with just four wins in the last 17 league games of the season, Sunderland once again ended up seventh, again just missing out on European football. As in the season before, it was a more than respectable position, overachievement even, but if they'd spent those two seasons dallying around in mid-table before making a late run for Europe, they'd have been praised to the hilt. Instead they bottled it, throwing away a valuable top four position before slithering down the league out of European contention.

There were reasons both on and off the field why Sunderland floundered again when they had so much to play for. Firstly, the goals had started to dry up for Kevin Phillips. He'd scored against Ipswich Town on New Years Day 2001, but only managed one more league goal between then and the beginning of May. With the side overly reliant on him to get goals, results took a turn for the worse and with the ageing Niall Quinn's powers beginning to wane, Sunderland were crying out for a fresh goal supply.

Don Hutchison had a tremendous season and seemed to have some involvement in practically every goal Sunderland scored, but he was the best thing about an unsettled midfield which was seriously wanting when compared to the First Division winning middle men from two years prior. Kevin Kilbane had failed to settle and was utterly bereft of confidence – Sunderland's slide the year before had started when he had arrived and the boo-boys were on his back whenever he stepped on to the pitch. Julio Arca had raw talent, but was young and needed time to develop, while Stefan Schwarz was a shadow of the player he'd been the year before.

Phillips didn't help matters for himself. Puffed-up from earning his international honours, he spoke mysteriously in interviews of wanting to develop his all-round game, and spent more time dropping deep to link up the play between midfield and attack. Sunderland fans didn't want Phillips to have an all-round game – as an out-and-out striker he was one of the best in the country, a 'fox in the box' with an unerring natural eye for goal. They didn't want him to become some kind of third-rate Dennis Bergkamp. Sadly, whether it was instigated by Reid, England boss Kevin Keegan or Phillips himself, Super Kev was never the same player again.

Off the field, Sunderland did nothing to strengthen their hand when they were sitting in second place in January 2001. One or two key signings at that time could have lifted the club into the upper echelons of the Premiership for good, but they never came, because Bob Murray or Peter Reid were either unable or unwilling to take the leap. Around that time, Murray uttered his famous phrase 'when Peter Reid leaves so do I', which was foolish at the time and looks even more foolish with hindsight. The chairman, blinded into believing that the good times would last forever, should have realised that even with the team pushing for a European place, all was not well. A favourite phrase of Peter Reid's was 'if you stand still in football you start going backwards.' He'd have done well to follow his own advice.

CHAPTER EIGHT

GETTING IT RIGHT?

WITH THE HALFWAY stage of the season rapidly approaching, Roy Keane had made a less than spectacular start to his career as a manager. Fans who had expected him to storm the club and instantly mould a footballing superpower out a team of underachievers with a confidence problem were sorely disappointed. Sure, results had improved from the start of the season when Niall Quinn had reluctantly worn the manager's hat but it was now November, and Sunderland were still floundering, searching for a run of form that could prevent the whole season from becoming consolidation, just an exercise in treading water. Quinn's magic carpet ride was spluttering and experiencing some mid-air turbulence.

Sitting in 19th, the Wearsiders' main failings were obvious – silly mistakes were being made in defence while at the other end of the pitch, there was a major problem with the productivity of the team's forwards. In the first 17 league matches, the side had produced the less-than-spectacular sum of 21 goals.

The top scorer was Chris Brown – and he had scored just three times, which meant that encouragingly, the goals were coming from throughout the whole team. But it definitely wasn't promotion form, or anything like it.

There were further departures from the Stadium of Light as Roy Keane whittled down his squad and shipped out those who he felt weren't going to be a part of his future plans. In most cases he was diplomatic, trotting out familiar-sounding lines about how the players in question would benefit from some first-team football and that a temporary move would be best if it would allow them to get that regular action. But in truth, it was improbable that the likes of Clive Clarke, Neill Collins and Rory Delap would be returning to force their way into the starting line-up on Wearside.

Tommy Miller was the latest player to depart, with Preston North End his new temporary home. So much had been expected of Miller when he signed for Sunderland in the summer of 2005; a local lad, a born and bred Sunderland fan, he had been a regular goal-scorer for Ipswich Town in the Championship and it was felt he could comfortably make the step up to the top flight, chipping in with a few goals along the way. It didn't turn out like that at all – Miller was quickly dubbed 'The Invisible Man' by supporters and his three goals in 33 league appearances fell way short of what was expected. Miller himself later complained that he'd been deployed in a deeper role than he was used to, but whatever had gone on the season before, the fact was that Keane had jettisoned the midfielder from his first-team squad soon after arriving on Wearside. The move to Preston was to be Miller's only realistic chance of getting any match action in the near future.

The identity of the second player to go out on loan was more surprising. Liam Lawrence had been part of the first team during the season so far, although his performances were riddled with inconsistency. The incident which led to the move was an alleged training-ground bust-up between Lawrence and Keane after the former was substituted during a full-scale practice match. Word was that Lawrence had trudged off to the changing room to get changed, but had been hauled back by his manager and made to watch the remainder of the game from the touchline. The row spilled over once the training session had ended, and within days, Lawrence was on his way to Stoke City on loan, with a view to a permanent move the following January. Rule one – you do it Keane's way or risk the consequences.

Liam Lawrence was a player who had been laughably compared by some to David Beckham, but the only real similarities between the pair are that they both play on the right-hand side of midfield, have no real pace to speak of and that they both seem to be overly fond of hair care. Beckham's lack of pace is countered by his pinpoint passing and crossing abilities, whereas Lawrence has very little else in his locker to make up for his shortcomings – apart, presumably, from expensive shampoo. Lawrence had been popular with the supporters, particularly during the promotion campaign of 2004–05, but the fans had gradually fallen out of love with him, and a move was surely in the best interests of all parties.

Another fans' favourite who had underachieved returned to the starting line-up in the next match, at home to Colchester United, which incredibly was the first time the two clubs had ever met. Stephen Elliott had hit the ground running when he arrived at Sunderland from Manchester City, at roughly the same time as Lawrence. The Irish under 21 international was an instant hit, scoring nine times in his first 20 matches, although as Sunderland climbed the table that season, and eventually won the Championship, the goals dried up for him as he scored just seven in his final 27 games. Not the form of a top-class striker, particularly one in a team that was winning games more often than not and heading for the top of the league.

Elliott's strike rate was worse still in the Premiership horror season of 2005–06, scoring just twice in 16 appearances in what was an injury-blighted campaign for the player. Whatever else he'll achieve at Sunderland or elsewhere, he'll always be fondly remembered for the scorching goal he scored against Newcastle at St James' Park in a game which Sunderland ultimately lost. They lost a lot of games that year. It's a sore point.

Having spent the previous couple of months struggling with various injuries, Elliott was keen to make his mark on the club's faltering season, and the Colchester game was the first time he would start a game since Roy Keane's arrival back in August. His return would provide an instant remedy for Sunderland's goal-scoring problems.

Elsewhere against Colchester, Keane seemed no nearer to determining who his first choice right-back would be, with Dean Whitehead getting another chance in the troublesome role. Typically, further changes were made, with Connolly and Caldwell both dropping to the bench, and Stan Varga given another chance at the back. Elliott took his place on the right flank in a 4-5-1/4-3-3 line-up and the change of formation led to a rough, disjointed first half; the players struggled to adapt to the change of shape and a string of misplaced passes soon had the crowd vocalising their frustration and impatience.

It was right on the cusp of half-time, just as fans began streaming towards the concourses in search of alcoholic enlightenment, that Elliott regained his knack for finding the back of the net. Receiving the ball just outside the right of the penalty area from Dean Whitehead, Elliott turned his defender and touched the ball into the box before hitting a firm shot with the outside of his right foot, sending it bending away from Colchester 'keeper Aidan Davison and in off the post.

With their half-time pints tasting that little bit sweeter, the fans' still-jangling nerves were settled further on 53 minutes when Elliott doubled his tally for the afternoon, dispatching a simple tap-in after Dean Whitehead had taken the ball to the right-hand bye-line before cutting it back for the Irishman.

So far so good, but nobody had expected Colchester to be a walkover – the visitors were hovering on the cusp of the play-off places and they gradually played their way back into the match, scoring with 11 minutes remaining as they were aided by some feeble Sunderland defending. As the ball pinged in and around their area, the home side had ample opportunity to put a boot through it and clear the danger but it eventually fell to Chris Iwelumo who put it in the back of the net from eight yards.

Sunderland reverted to panic mode once more and Colchester sensed that an equaliser was there for the taking if they piled the pressure on to Sunderland's creaking back line. Hearts were in mouths when Jamie Cureton (who would finish the season as the league's top scorer) broke through and found himself one on one with Darren Ward. Cureton lofted the ball above the reach of Ward but thankfully, the striker's golden touch had deserted him as the ball kept rising, up and over the bar.

The three points were sealed right at the death when Kavanagh sent a delicate ball into the box which substitute David Connolly skilfully brought down. For a player who was coming to the end of his tenth Sunderland appearance without a goal, he might have been expected to try a snap shot and hope for the best, but Connolly showed his class and composure, taking a couple of touches to steady himself and work an angle from where he could shoot. Surprisingly, there was no challenge from the surrounding Colchester defenders and Connolly was almost allowed a free shot. It looked easier than it was, but he put the ball in the corner of Davison's net with the 'keeper either unsighted or wrong-footed.

Connolly was finally off the mark for his new club, and the win which had eluded the Black Cats since the last-minute show at Hull was theirs, giving them a little breathing space between themselves and the danger zone. Afterwards, Roy Keane's assessment was, 'As usual, we made it very hard for ourselves,' although some observers would have argued with his assertion that 'in parts of the game we were really good – outstanding. We passed it and moved it well.' Not in the first half they didn't.

David Connolly revealed his relief at finally getting that all-important first goal, while speaking of the frustration he'd endured on his way to getting it. He told the club website, 'Things haven't quite fallen for me since I came to the club. There haven't been any tap-ins or anything. If I keep hitting the target I am sure the goals will keep coming.'

All eyes immediately turned to the following week's fixture – an away game at Wolverhampton Wanderers, and the long-awaited public meeting of Roy Keane and Mick McCarthy. Even the news that Clive Clarke's loan spell at Coventry had been extended was met with little or no celebration on Wearside, such was the anticipation of the titanic clash that lay ahead the following Friday evening. One bookmaker was offering odds of 100/1 against Keane punching his former international boss at some point, which was ridiculous. These men are professionals, and 150/1 would have been more realistic.

McCarthy appeared more than ready to bury the hatchet and put an end to the turbulence of the past four years, saying, 'Four years on, I was man enough to make a call to Roy Keane recently and he was gracious enough to take it. We both did what we thought was right at the time during the 2002 World Cup and we have made our peace with each other. There will be a handshake and we will get on with it.' Bad news for those who hoped to see the pair brawling on the Molineux touchline.

When the long-awaited moment finally arrived, McCarthy sought out Keane, who was standing his ground by his dugout technical area, the Wolves boss scampering across with a small army of photographers in his wake. The handshake from McCarthy was warm, and Keane duly obliged, but he looked impassive and unimpressed by it all, maintaining his mask of indifference as McCarthy stopped short of going for an all-out conciliatory bear hug. Keane was unlikely to have joined in if he had. One thing would be certain – if there was any match this season where Keane would want to come out of it unbeaten then this was the one.

Uncharacteristically, Keane made just one change to the starting line-up that had faced Colchester, David Connolly replacing Chris Brown, presumably earning a start on the back of his first goal for the club. Keane persisted with the lone striker formation, but the side who he thought were outstanding in the previous match were anything but during the first half in the Black Country.

Sunderland failed to stamp any sort of authority on the match, with Wolves dominating in midfield, and only a string of top-class saves from Darren Ward kept them in the game. Fittingly, when Ward's defences were finally breached, it was from a wonder goal from Wolves' Jemal Johnson, one that separated the sides at half-time. Johnson picked up the ball 25 yards out and some sloppy marking from Danny Collins afforded him the time and space to crack a shot which rose and rose, evading Ward's desperate dive and rattling the back of the net. Sunderland could have no complaints, and without Ward's inspired contribution, they could have been at least three down by the break.

Tobias Hysen was brought on at half-time, in place of Yorke, who had been curiously off the pace since the start. The change meant that Sunderland could revert to a more familiar 4-4-2, but it was almost in vain midway through the second half, when Wolves had a chance to wrap up the game that was as golden as their shirts. Leon Clarke found himself completely unmarked and just eight yards from goal; astonishingly his shot was blocked by Darren Ward and McCarthy must have rued the chance for him to wrap up the post-match bragging rights.

Sunderland escaped from the match with a point and Keane escaped with his pride reasonably intact, their equaliser mirroring the goal they had conceded against Colchester six days before. The ball bobbled around Wolves' box, with the home side unable to get a decisive contact on it that would enable them to lash it to safety. It fell to Stephen Elliott, who had drifted out unmarked to the left-hand side of the box. His shot was mis-hit and seemed to make its way towards Matt Murray's goal line in slow motion but it eventually crossed the line and gave the Wearsiders a point which they genuinely didn't deserve but which saw them hold on to 16th place.

On either side of the Wolves trip, Keane indulged in some goalkeeper swapping. With Ben Alnwick out injured, Marton Fulop, a giant Hungarian international, came on loan from Tottenham Hotspur as cover. However, within a few days, Alnwick himself went the other way, signing for Spurs for £1 million, with Fulop's short-term Wearside stay becoming permanent as part of the deal.

With barely any chance to pause for breath, Sunderland faced another away match. A midweek trip to Queens Park Rangers represented a major expedition for players and fans alike, but it was a worthwhile one as Sunderland collected all three points and extended their unbeaten run to four matches.

From the first kick, Sunderland were in a different league to the home team, the 4-5-1 system working for once as the wide men grafted tirelessly in both attack and defence, and the Black Cats took the lead on 17 minutes. A deep corner from Kavanagh was cleared as far as Grant Leadbitter and the youngster's shot travelled through a morass of bodies in the penalty box until it reached Daryl Murphy, whose stooping header diverted it beyond QPR's 'keeper Royce. To a man, the QPR players appealed for an offside, and Murphy hesitantly looked to the referee's assistant, but the flag wasn't lifted and the goal celebrations commenced.

Afterwards, Sunderland strove to attack again and again, looking to puncture Rangers' fragile defence at every opportunity. Their momentum was only halted midway through the half when an enraged QPR fan saw fit to throw a plastic bottle at the referee's assistant as Sunderland prepared to take a corner. Exuberant referee Uriah Rennie came bounding across and at one point it seemed as though he wasn't going to allow the game to continue until the culprit had been identified, interviewed and DNA tested. Eventually, the demonstrative official settled for an increased number of stewards in front of the section of crowd from where the missile had originated, and normal service was resumed.

Rennie had refereed at Deepdale the previous Saturday, and had been at his self-aggrandising best, so much so that the Preston tannoy announcer amused everyone at half-time by hailing 'the second half of The Uriah Rennie Show.' Everyone, that is, except Rennie himself, who not surprisingly is a magistrate in his spare time.

Sunderland's second goal came deep into the first half stoppage time that had led from the plastic bottle incident, and there was another offside shout in the build up to it. A neat ball was slipped through the QPR back line by Liam Miller to Grant Leadbitter, who didn't look back, racing on towards Simon Royce before calmly stroking the ball around the 'keeper and into the back of the net.

The second half started as a direct continuation of the first. Kavanagh, Miller and Leadbitter had outplayed the home side in the middle of the park throughout, but the latter pair were substituted within six minutes of each other, possibly to keep them fresh for the next fixture, but the changes were a mistake and Sunderland lost their way once two of the cogs from their midfield machine had been removed.

Accordingly, on 73 minutes, QPR got back into a game in which they should have been given no chance with a consolation goal from Ray Jones, again with a hint of offside about it, creating yet another tense end to a Sunderland match. The Wearsiders seemed unfazed by Rangers' impudence and pressed on to try and finish off their opponents, but left themselves exposed at the back at the same time. Sunderland spurned three gilt-edged chances to ease their supporters' worries in the dying minutes, and Ross Wallace would probably suffer from a week or two of night terrors as he recalled slicing a shot wide of an open goal, a mistake that was almost unfairly punished when Darren Ward was forced into making an exceptional save in the last minute.

Thankfully, the match ended 2-1, and Sunderland had bagged themselves another three points, but Keane wasn't afraid to confess that the last ten minutes had been 'bloody hell down on the bench.' The same must have applied for his opposite number, as John Gregory initially declined to speak to the press, crying off with a splitting headache before making an appearance a little later, presumably after a couple of aspirins.

Four points from two consecutive away games was more like the form Sunderland were aiming for, and their performances away from the Stadium of Light were becoming more fruitful than those at home. One impressive performance on the road that had earned them nothing had been at Norwich just a month before, and a quirk in the fixture list gave the Wearsiders a swift opportunity to get revenge when the Canaries came to the north east on December 2nd.

There were the customary changes to the line-up – just two this time, with Whitehead reverting to right-back, and the 4-5-1 formation being given another run out after its success in West London. Trouble was, the football at QPR was at times a delight to watch, the game back on home soil was a morbid, turgid, tortuous 90 minutes. A horrible example of what is sometimes laughably called 'the beautiful game.' Hindered by the rapidly deteriorating pitch and the Stadium of Light's traditional wind, which always seems to know when Sunderland are playing at home and duly acts accordingly, a 1-0 win was as good as it was ever going to get for either side.

But it was one of those scrappy, ugly wins which can be just as, if not more, satisfying than a stylish, comprehensive victory – especially when every point was crucial, as was now becoming the case for Sunderland with their move up the table starting to make other managers take an unsure look over their shoulders.

The only goal came from one of the game's rare slick and assured moves, the ball travelling from Darren Ward to the back of the Norwich net, courtesy of a few well-chosen passes which ended up at the feet of Daryl Murphy. Murphy received the ball on the edge of the penalty area with his back to goal, spun and hit a first-time shot low past the 'keeper's right hand. There was just under a quarter of an hour left, and in truth Norwich never looked like getting back into the game after that.

Murphy was slowly becoming a more confident and imposing figure while leading the line on his own, and some of the fist-in-mouth performances he had put in earlier in the season were gradually being erased from memory. Despite that, his display against Norwich was not one of his best, but the important statistic is the one under the scoreline where his name was.

The supporters may have been taking their frustrations out on the players the longer it took Sunderland to break the deadlock, but Roy Keane pointed out just how relaxed he had been on the day. 'I just had a good feeling about it,' he said afterwards. 'I got up and had a good breakfast, a nice bacon and egg sandwich, and I just felt good about the game, I was very relaxed about the whole thing.'

With Luton heading north the following weekend, it meant two consecutive Saturdays with matches at the

Stadium of Light. A couple of minor matters filled up the intervening days – the draw for the third round of the FA Cup, which sent Sunderland back to Preston North End again, and a minor tabloid scandal.

The Sun revealed that four current and former players had starred in a sex tape which included a girl who later turned out to be 16 years old.

Of the players involved, Martin Woods had left the club in the summer, while Ben Alnwick and Liam Lawrence were halfway out of the door. Only Chris Brown remained, although it wouldn't be for long. Brown had previously made his way into the wrong half of the papers when he was arrested following an incident during which a ballbearing gun was fired at passers-by from a moving car.

Who knows, maybe his targets were Sunderland fans, the people who were paying his wages. One can only imagine Niall Quinn's reaction – he'd spoken of his desire to reconnect the club with its fans, although this was probably not quite what he had in mind.

The Luton match produced Sunderland's first truly convincing home performance since Sheffield Wednesday, which had been over two months earlier. The Hatters headed into the match in a tailspin, having lost seven of their previous eight games. They were hurtling down the table after a bright start to the season.

Among the line-up changes, Marton Fulop appeared in goal for the first time, replacing the injured Darren Ward, and doubts about his suitability were raised when Luton went ahead in less than five minutes, Dean Morgan's low shot rebounded off Stan Varga for Morgan to finish the job off properly.

Sunderland quickly restored parity, Daryl Murphy continuing his hot streak of goalscoring form with his third in as many games four minutes later. Bundling the ball away from a dithering Luton defender on the left-hand side, Murphy charged into the box before smashing the ball up into the top corner of the net from an acute angle.

That the game only finished 2-1 was a surprise considering the amount of goalmouth action there was at each end. It was David Connolly who wrapped up the points with a classy winning goal after 53 minutes. The striker received the ball on the edge of the box and with his back to goal and within a split second he had turned and driven a low shot past the Luton 'keeper.

There had been the beginnings of some dissent coming from the less enlightened factions of the team's followers due to Connolly's lack of goals, but during his barren early spell, the striker never hid and his all-round contribution had been a key part of the team's cause. After the Luton game, the player would never look back as he hit a three-month golden streak.

Afterwards, both managers claimed their team deserved the points, but the facts were there for all to see. Six matches unbeaten now, and as the year drew to a close Sunderland's yo-yo season was beginning to take a more positive turn. But two away games in the space of three days could make or break their season...

CHAPTER NINE

CHRISTMAS AND THE SPIRIT OF GIVING

The Luton game coincided with the advent of Roy Keane's first 100 days as a manager and the win was a good indicator of how far Sunderland had come in the three months or so since the new manager first sent a team out on to the park at Derby. In August the thought that the red and whites would be piecing together a six-game unbeaten run was laughable. Back then, under Niall Quinn they were lucky to go six minutes without coming close to conceding a goal. The Irishman took over a side littered with players who were actually afraid to play football – players who were unwilling to try something that wasn't in the game's basic handbook in case they slipped up and the consequences led to yet another goal conceded or a barracking from the terraces.

Keane's first job was to get those players reminding themselves that they were professional footballers and that they had an inherent ability and a right to do what opposition players were doing against them week in and week out. Crucial too was the introduction of a smattering of new faces, players who hadn't been saddled with the losing mentality, who didn't come to work each day with a cloud hanging over them. Dwight Yorke was probably Keane's most important signing, a man blessed with boundless enthusiasm who conveniently also knows how to pass a ball around. Yorke was the shot in the arm that the squad needed, and it was quickly apparent that Keane was overseeing a happier camp, with everyone working together as a team.

There were smaller changes that had wider significance too. Probably because of the differences in the standards of preparation he'd experienced with Manchester United and the Republic of Ireland, Keane was quick to ensure that his players received the best possible treatment ahead of match days. The squad now spent the night before every match together in a hotel, home or away. A blend of obsessive control and five-star treatment removed some of the variables that could later be blamed if something were to go wrong on a match day. The benefits in terms of team harmony were becoming more apparent as the 100 day anniversary passed by with results on an upswing.

There were still situations that needed to be addressed – Keane was a long way from settling on a fixed back four, but the transfer window was fast approaching and he'd have a month to put that right. Plus they were still shy of a regular goal scorer, but the Championship needn't be a hard league to get out of if you've got a system you believe in and a bunch of hard-working players with a touch of flair in there to set you apart from the rest of the drones. Sunderland didn't quite have that magic formula yet, but it was clear that they were working towards it – the six game unbeaten run was proof of that.

On the back of that run, and with the festive season approaching, Sunderland's steadily-improving team found themselves with four matches remaining for 2006, two at home and two away. Crucially, they all felt winnable and the new year, coinciding with the re-opening of the transfer window could be looking very promising indeed. Although the side were moving only slowly up the table, in terms of points on the board, the Wearsiders were creeping up on those teams who were jockeying for a play-off berth, sitting just three points behind sixth-placed Southampton.

As the transfer window was preparing to open again, Keane and Sunderland were beginning to be linked with some interesting names. Most of the rumours were best taken with a pinch of salt – as it was common knowledge that Drumaville had cash to spend, the club were always going to seem like an easy target for predatory agents.

Even with that in mind, the fact that names like David Beckham and Ole Gunnar Solskjaer were being linked with Wearside was incredible for a club who had been scraping around at the bottom of the barrel for recruits just a year or so before.

Of course, Beckham and Solskjaer were never remotely likely to come – as Roy Keane said himself, 'A lot of this is just agents talking up potential moves to get themselves an early Christmas present. I don't want to go down that road.' Plus, Drumaville's members would surely baulk at trying to match the $50 million dollars that Golden Balls will be trousering if he sees out his five-year contract with LA Galaxy. Keane's targets were more likely to be the kind of player who could fit into his existing system and improve the team, helping them towards the immediate goal of getting out of the Championship. Anything else would be folly and showmanship – not the kind of words that you'd usually associate with Roy Keane.

One name that kept cropping up was that of Anthony Stokes. The young striker had called in at the Academy of Light for a short trial in July 2006, during Niall Quinn's mercifully brief managerial reign. Quinn had decided that Stokes wasn't significantly better than the club already had and sent him on his way. The lad continued northwards and ended up landing a five-month loan spell with Falkirk, where he scored 14 goals in 16 SPL games, including a hat-trick of hat-tricks.

Now that Stokes' loan deal was coming to an end, he was being touted around as Arsenal looked to cash in on a player Arsene Wenger didn't believe would make it in North London. Keane was making positive noise regarding lining up a deal for Stokes, but he'd have some stiff competition – Celtic had already had a £700,000 offer rejected by Arsenal, and the SPL champions were putting together an improved offer.

As for Keane's other targets, he was keeping them close to his chest, which is arguably the best way to do business in football. Announce a name before you've done the deal and you run the risk of ending up with egg on your face. It happened to Sunderland back in 2002, when the club proudly announced they'd agreed a fee with Leeds United for Robbie Keane, only for the player to have a think and decide that he didn't fancy it all that much.

But potential new recruits would have to go on the back burner for a couple of weeks as the Black Cats concentrated on reaping a few more points for the Championship campaign. Burnley manager Steve Cotterill, Howard Wilkinson's number two during the turmoil-riddled post-Peter Reid era in 2002, would have been particularly keen to get one over on the club where he felt unfairly and prematurely dismissed before Mick McCarthy was given the job. The Clarets were sitting in seventh and although they wouldn't be a pushover, Sunderland would be expecting to put on a display and try and extend that unbeaten run a little further.

On the team sheet, Darren Ward returned in goal and the midfield saw two changes, with Grant Leadbitter and Dwight Yorke coming in for Graham Kavanagh and Liam Miller. Keane continued to persist with Stephen Elliott as a right-winger, back in a more familiar 4-4-2 on this occasion, but it was surely only a short-term stopgap role – some genuine pace and creativity was needed down the right-hand side.

Shortly after the kick-off, it seemed as though only one team had actually bothered to turn up and put in any real effort and it wasn't Sunderland. As had happened far too many times in recent weeks, Sunderland fell behind to an early goal.

As a defensive unit, the side were starting to show a distinct improvement from the kamikaze early days of the season but the nasty habit of conceding early goals was only making the task of climbing the table that much harder.

Again, at Burnley, less than ten minutes had been played when Sunderland fell behind. Kyle Lafferty got on the end of a quick Clarets' counter-attack and comfortably slotted the ball past Ward before Sunderland's midfielders had had a chance to figure out what was going on and react accordingly. Following the goal, Sunderland slowly fought their way back into contention but an equaliser failed to arrive and the visitors were buckling again when the referee blew for half-time.

Dwight Yorke got himself an assist seven minutes after the break, but unfortunately it was in the build-up to Burnley's second goal. His backwards defensive header was devoid of any power or direction and simply dropped into the path of Lafferty again, the teenager hitting a first-time shot from the edge of the box straight past Ward and into the back of the net.

By now, the 3,500-strong travelling red and white army were resigning themselves to the fact that they'd made another fruitless away trip – Sunderland hadn't played particularly badly but both goals had stemmed from unforced individual errors, the bane of Sunderland's season so far.

It wasn't too long before Keane made changes. Dwight Yorke, whose poor performance had been compounded by his mistake for Burnley's second goal, was replaced by Liam Miller. On the left wing Graham Kavanagh came on for Ross Wallace, Daryl Murphy drifting out to the left-hand side, and Grant Leadbitter pushed further forward to support Connolly.

Shortly afterwards, Murphy, too, was taken off and replaced by Toby Hysen, restoring the 4-5-1 system that had become the norm in previous weeks. Sunderland began to improve and looked more fluid having reverted to 4-5-1, pushing the wide men on again into 4-3-3 when going forward.

It all fell into place with ten minutes to play. With the Black Cats fans congregated behind the goal, Grant Leadbitter picked up the ball from Elliott, made himself a yard of space outside the box before firing home a sweet shot, giving Sunderland a slender hope of recovery.

Burnley had a sure-fire opportunity to put the game beyond Sunderland's reach three minutes later, Caldwell making a great challenge as Jones prepared to shoot from eight yards. The Clarets would be left to heavily rue the miss as Sunderland, sensing an opportunity continued to fight their way back into the game.

Like Hull, it was another late, late spectacular for the travelling fans. The equaliser finally came two minutes into added time, Ward humping a long hopeful ball forward which was headed on in the direction of David Connolly. The striker let it bounce before letting rip from well outside the area to clinch a vital point and extend the Wearsiders' unbeaten run to seven games.

It was Connolly's third goal for the club and he raced straight over to the crowd, some of whom had spilled out of the stand and on to the side of the pitch. The striker later said, 'I thought if I scored at Burnley that I would do it. I went to them and it was worth a booking.'

As a man who was forced to watch from the sidelines as his Manchester United teammates pulled off the impossible 1999 Champions League victory, Roy Keane knows the value of a comeback, and Burnley left him with mixed feelings – while he was disappointed with the overall performance, he praised his players for sticking at it right until the end, saying, 'You can never give a game of football up, there's plenty of examples of teams coming back. You keep going until the end.'

It would be unthinkable that the team that lost at Southend and Bury in the first month of the season could have pulled off a recovery like the one at Burnley, and although they came away from Turf Moor with just a point, the way they battled and scrapped in order to earn it made the trip to Burnley one of the most significant matches in Sunderland's season. Their willingness to persevere when all appeared lost, added to the physical effort required to dig out a result like that, would stand Sunderland in good stead as the season dragged on. There would be plenty more battling and scrapping required if they were to get out of this league at the first attempt, especially when it came to facing Burnley again towards the end of the season.

The run came to an end three days before Christmas at the home of Crystal Palace. It was a Friday night match, moved for Sky TV, and nothing about it felt right. Sunderland fans faced a long and arduous round-trip now that the fixture had been moved back from the Saturday afternoon, and was so inconveniently close to the festive season. Additionally, Selhurst Park was draped in a thick fog long before the game got underway, and there were real doubts that it should have been played at all.

Nyron Nosworthy returned at right-back allowing Dean Whitehead to revert to his regular midfield role, and Kavanagh and Miller also returned as Keane played musical midfielders once again. Crystal Palace came into the game with just two wins from their previous 14 games and with the threat of the sack hanging over manager Peter Taylor's head.

For all of Sunderland's clever passing and ball retention, the game ended up as yet another glaring lesson in what the side were lacking as opposed to what they actually had. The fog didn't help, with it being impossible to see from one end of the pitch to the other for most of the time, but Sunderland easily controlled the first half without ever penetrating the Palace defence. Once again, Connolly's movement pulled defenders out of position but the midfielders were rarely able or willing to get forward and exploit the space.

Against the run of play, the Eagles took the lead four minutes from the end of the first half, Mark Hudson driving a shot past Ward after Shefki Kuqi headed into his path. The second half differed little from the first, which made it all the more infuriating. Time and time again, Sunderland advanced into promising positions before failing to capitalise on the advantage and test Palace's 'keeper Julian Speroni. Substitutions were made with little effect, and the visitors' best chance came when Stan Varga forced Speroni to tip his header over the bar towards the end.

It was scandalous that Sunderland should come out of the match with nothing for their efforts, but effort was all they offered on the night. The manager was not amused – his observations were pointed and accurate, saying, 'Clearly, some of our players aren't ready for the next challenge, and that makes it so frustrating.'

He was well aware of the lacklustre way in which his players continued to operate when in attacking positions, adding, 'You've got to take risks in football, especially in the attacking third. We got into too many decent positions and we ended up going back towards our goal, and that's no good to us. If they keep going back to the 'keeper, then they will be criticised – because anyone can do that, and we don't want that at Sunderland.'

It was a stark reminder to the players that the transfer window would be opening soon and Keane was ready to throw one or two of them out of it if improvements weren't forthcoming.

He was at his best again a couple of days later ahead of the Boxing Day clash with Leeds United, warning the players not to ruin the holiday season for the fans, saying, 'We'll have a big crowd in and they'll be expecting us to react positively. They'll want to leave with smiles on their faces. The players have to go out and enjoy playing in front of the big crowd. It should be why they wanted to be footballers.'

The manager's empathy with the feelings of the paying public was doing him no harm whatsoever, and there'd be more than one occasion during the season when he'd describe his job as helping the fans to enjoy their Saturday night pints that bit more.

With just one point one from the past two games, a win over Leeds would be essential if Sunderland were to get back on the track towards the play-offs. Since the 3-0 win at Elland Road in early September, there'd been a change of management, with Dennis Wise taking over from the deposed Kevin Blackwell. With both Wise and Ken Bates at the club, the reasons to dislike Leeds United were starting to stack up and it would be hard to find a neutral who would sympathise with their increasingly desperate battle against relegation.

A massive crowd of 40,116 was the third largest in the country on the day (only Manchester United and Chelsea attracted more), but if many of them were only irregular visitors to the Stadium of Light, there was very little on show in the first hour that would have them signing up for the part-season tickets that had recently gone on sale.

After 60 minutes of utter dross, Sunderland made the breakthrough and their opening goal was a delight to watch. Yorke threaded a sublime through-pass to Connolly who still had a lot of work to do as he took it down the right-hand edge of the penalty area. He reached the bye-line before jinking back on himself, leaving the defender twisting and turning. Connolly kept his shot low, ensuring that it evaded the covering defenders and the 'keeper, and Sunderland were finally a goal to the good after 65 minutes.

That goal knocked the wind out of the visitors' sails and the Wearsiders inevitably scored again ten minutes from the end. Grant Leadbitter put the points beyond Leeds' grasp, nicking the ball from Daryl Murphy's feet as the big Irishman tried to find an opening for a shot on the edge of the box. The youngster appeared from midfield and took it on, hitting the ball crisply first time from the edge of the area. Two–nil.

There was even time for some high comedy. Earlier, the Leeds bench had been enraged when one of their rare attacking moves was pulled back by the referee when a ballboy mistakenly allowed a second ball to bounce onto the pitch. Minutes later, with Sunderland pressing forward, Leeds' assistant boss Gus Poyet helped another stray ball onto the field, hoping that the referee would stop play again. When the official did stop the game, his first action was to head towards Poyet and show him the red card. Dirty Leeds?

Keane was pleased with the result and the attendance, describing the turn-out as 'Brilliant. But I've played here with 49,000 slagging me off. I know the potential.' The win didn't lift Sunderland any further up the table but they remained in eleventh, just three points shy of the play-off zone and a tempting seven away from automatic promotion. An end of season reward was looking a distinct possibility – the team would need to knuckle down and find some consistency from hereon in. If they could do that, there could be no stopping them.

Preston North End arrived for the final game of 2006 – the year that had seemed to last forever. It had probably been the weirdest 12 months in the history of Sunderland Association Football Club. Four managers, a match abandoned due to a freak Easter blizzard, relegation with a new record low points tally, the sale of the club to a legendary former player and his unassuming consortium of Irish businessmen, the promise of a world class manager followed quickly by the appointment of a rookie, and all the football that had followed.

Now Preston were in town and a chance came to avenge the 4-1 defeat at Deepdale from earlier in the season. But North End were a tough, well-organised side who were nudging at an automatic promotion place, and a significant overall improvement on the Leeds performance would be needed.

Injuries, particularly in defence, were beginning to take their toll, with Nosworthy chosen to play at left-back while Nyatanga, who had been filling that role, was left on the bench. It all righted itself when Caldwell went off injured after 16 minutes and the Derby loanee came into the fray.

Once again, Sunderland frustrated a decent-sized home support with their shot-shy approach in front of goal and paid for it with a 1-0 defeat. The home side had the lion's share of possession throughout but couldn't convert it into goals. At the other end, Preston had the trump card in David Nugent, a striker who had got into the habit of scoring the goals that had propelled his side up the table.

He nodded in the game's only goal from two yards out in the 36th minute as Sunderland's back line stood around and watched him, Nosworthy in particular seemingly incapable of jumping and getting a connection onto the cross from Brett Ormerod. It was Preston's only real chance of the match. Sunderland had many more but couldn't convert them. It didn't take a genius to figure out where the problem lay.

The treatment room gained a couple of new residents too – Nyron Nosworthy picked up a hamstring strain to add to Caldwell's thigh injury which saw him limp off during the game. Danny Collins, Stephen Wright and Kenny Cunningham were in there waiting for them.

As the last game of 2006 passed by with no reward, it was time for Keane to shuffle his pack as the transfer window opened. There were no two ways about it – Sunderland's season would live or die depending on the success of the manager's wheeling and dealing.

Roy Keane's last visit to the Stadium of Light before he took over as manager. Niall Quinn tries to act as peacemaker as Sir Alex Ferguson turns puce and Keane completes his sending off.

*Peter Reid with Niall Quinn and daughter after Sunderland's record-
shattering Division 1 title win of 1999, won in a stylish, comprehensive
manner that will never be forgotten.*

Kevin Phillips trudges off after Sunderland's relegation is confirmed in 2003.
Their 19 points that season would be a record low – until 2006's
15-point disgrace.

What's wrong with this picture? Old Gunnar Solskjaer wonders what is happening as Kelvin Davis celebrates a 0-0 draw at Old Trafford in April 2006. The result meant that Sunderland's relegation was certain.

Some 'intensive' dog walking after Roy Keane's surprise exit from Manchester United.

Niall Quinn, the chairman who sacked himself as manager so that Roy Keane could take over.

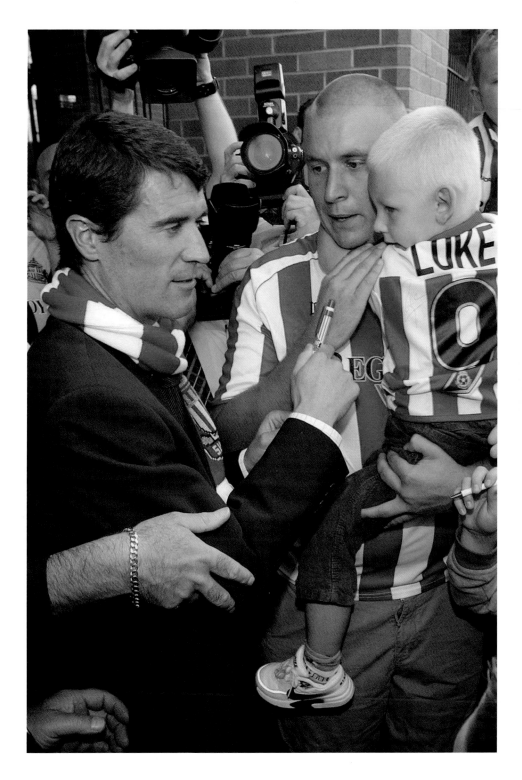

Young Luke becomes part of history when Roy Keane decides to become Sunderland boss.

Roy Keane with head coach Tony Loughlan during a training session at the Academy of Light training ground in Sunderland.

Not always calm. Roy Keane celebrates against Derby County.

Promotion gained and Roy Keane shows how to do it in the Premiership.

Homage!

Carlos Edwards hammers the third goal in the Burnley match.

Sunderland win the Championship and Nyron Nosworthy, turned into a central defender by Roy Keane, celebrates.

David Connolly celebrates his goal as Sunderland are ready to become champions by winning at Luton.

Keiran Richardson in the pre-season friendly with Bohemians.

The pre-season tour of Ireland, Roy Keane tells a young Bohemians supporter that management is a piece of cake.

CHAPTER TEN

A DECADE OF LIGHT
CHEER US UP
PETER REID

In the four years since it opened its shiny new turnstiles, pilgrims to the Stadium of Light had faithfully handed over their money and been rewarded with unrelenting success on the pitch. It started with two seasons of breathtaking football in the Football League First Division, and while promotion was missed by a whisker in the first year the job was done ruthlessly in the second.

Following that came two years of astonishing overachievement. Sunderland had been expected to be among those clubs frantically clambering on to their Premiership ticket when they got there in 1999 but 30 league goals from Kevin Phillips saw them finish seventh, a feat they repeated in the second season.

But it wasn't all rosy in the Wearside garden. Murmurings of discontent were emerging from the fan base. For the second season in a row, the team had been a whisker away from topping the Premiership only to fall away spectacularly in the second half of the season. Dissenters pointed to Peter Reid's inability to come up with a plan B when plan A wasn't working. Plan A, as anyone who just had a passing interest in football knew, was to get the ball up to Niall Quinn and let him hold it up or knock it down for Super Kevin Phillips to put into the net. It worked magnificently because Quinn was such a good player – he knew where to take up position, he was big, strong and a handful for defenders, plus he was very, very tasty when given the ball to feet, an added dimension for a 'target man'.

By 2001 however, Quinn's powers were on the wane and everyone knew it. The talisman was still some way from the end of his shelf-life, but a replacement would be needed sooner rather than later. More immediately, some help would be required as Quinn's recurring back problems meant it was practically impossible for him to last for the whole 90 minutes week in and week out.

Two seventh-placed finishes and week after week of sell-out crowds meant that Peter Reid once again had cash to spend. His big name buys had fluctuated between inspired and abominable. The manager couldn't be praised highly enough for picking up Kevin Phillips for £350,000 or Thomas Sorensen for £500,000, but over three million pounds had been spent on the duff duo of Carsten Fredgaard and Milton 'Tyson' Nunez, and both were still to start a league match since they arrived. In fact, Fredgaard left after two fruitless seasons, the club making a £1.2 million loss in exchange for one substitute league appearance.

Reid's recruits in the summer of 2001 were slightly eyebrow-raising as they were all unknown to the average football fan. The most notable was Lilian Laslandes, a striker with an impressive scoring record at club and international level in his native France. He arrived from Bordeaux for £3.6 million and looked set to be the eventual replacement for Niall Quinn, although at the age of 30, time was hardly on his side.

Following the success of Julio Arca, whom Reid had brought in the year before, the manager returned to plunder the Argentine under-21 side further, bringing midfielder Nicolas Medina to the north east for a fee of £3.5 million. Reid's other major signings that summer were Swiss right-back Bernt Haas (£750,000) and pacy striker David Bellion (free); each of them untested to the rigours of the English Premiership.

Sunderland suffered a hammer blow as the season got underway when Don Hutchison made it clear that he saw his future away from the Stadium of Light. Rumours circulated that the promise of a contract extension and pay increase led to nothing and within weeks, Hutch headed off to West Ham while Sunderland pocketed £5 million. It was a paltry compensation as Hutchison had been the fulcrum of Sunderland's midfield and in a season where Phillips didn't match his strike tally of the previous year, Hutchison's eight goals were much-needed, and the player added an extra dimension to the team's primary tactic of kicking it to Quinn.

The season started slowly and Sunderland failed to find any real consistency. From the very beginning it was obvious that Laslandes was struggling to adapt to the pace of the league or the Sunderland way of playing, and his exasperation was obvious at the barrage of high balls he was expected to win in the air, not a strong part of his game.

Quinn started the season on the bench with the Frenchman partnering Phillips, but the pair didn't gel and goals were scarce for the team. Phillips was doing his bit, scoring six times in his first ten matches, although it would take him the rest of the season to double that amount.

Laslandes lost his place after a month and Quinn was reinstated, although his best days had clearly gone. The other new signings were nothing to shout about either

– Bernt Haas had a long throw but that was about all, and Nicolas Medina got lost in the same part of the club that had swallowed up Fredgaard and Nunez. Although he turned out regularly in the reserves, the £3.5 million signing was nowhere to be seen when the first team were in action.

Sunderland were struggling to cope with the loss of Hutchison, and Reid inexplicably sold Alex Rae to Wolves before he'd even replaced Hutchison. While not the first name on the team sheet each week, Rae was a wholly-committed player. It would be another month, and two months after losing Hutchison, before Reid brought in any kind of replacement for the influential midfielder. Jason McAteer signed from Blackburn for a million pounds, but while he was a versatile, hard-working midfielder, he did not have same the craft about his game as the departed Hutchison.

With no sign of Medina's graduation to the first team in sight, Peter Reid splashed out another £4 million in December on Rangers' playmaker, the USA international captain Claudio Reyna. A player in much the same mould as Hutchison, strong and with a good passing range, he was just what Sunderland needed to strengthen their midfield.

Reyna had hardly had time to settle in when the New Year curse kicked in again. The only difference this time around was that they hadn't banked enough points before Christmas. Reid frequently said "if you stand still in football you go backwards", but in 2001 he'd put Sunderland into reverse gear and didn't seem to have a clue what to do about it.

Aware that Niall Quinn was running out of time and needed to be replaced, Reid brought in the Cameroon striker Patrick Mboma on loan from Parma. Mboma had been voted the African Player Of The Year in 2000, but the arrangement led many to question why Parma would be willing to loan him out in the first place if he was any good. He scored away at Tottenham in his first full start, but added nothing to Sunderland's floundering season and was usually withdrawn to make way for the old warhorse Quinn, with Sunderland invariably chasing the game. Eventually the roles were reversed and Quinn was restored to the first XI, with Mboma coming on when Quinn had exhausted himself.

The second half of the season was a slow death for Sunderland and three victories in their final 19 league games saw them slowly tumble down the league table again.

Their troubles were particularly acute when on their travels – during a run of nine away games, Sunderland lost eight of them, scoring just three times in total, a chronically bad run of results.

It was relegation form and by the final day of the season things had got so bad that there was a chance they could have fallen through the trapdoor at the last minute – if Ipswich had beaten Liverpool and the Black Cats had lost at home to Derby, Sunderland would have been relegated immediately after their best two seasons in decades. By scrapping their way to a dour 1-1 draw, Sunderland did enough to make sure that Ipswich's result didn't matter, but the rot had set in over the past few months and major surgery needed to be performed on the team. Matters weren't helped when Reid's number two, Bobby Saxton retired, but perhaps a change of personnel behind the scenes was needed. Coach Adrian Heath was promoted to assistant manager and Niall Quinn became a player-coach.

Quinn himself enjoyed a magnificent night at the Stadium of Light in May 2002 when his Republic of Ireland testimonial match was played there, his club side facing his national side. The genial forward raised in excess of a million pounds on the night, all of which was donated to charities in Sunderland and Ireland. Afterwards, Quinn headed off to the World Cup – Saipan, Keane, McCarthy and all.

Nobody could deny that Reid had worked miracles in the five years since the Stadium of Light opened, but he'd stuck to a rigid style of football in order to achieve that – the only problem was that he no longer had the players who were up to the task of effectively playing that way.

Buying Niall Quinn back in 1996 had been a genius piece of business, and building the team around the Irishman had brought nothing but success, but everything changes. Reid either couldn't or wouldn't see that, and the time had come for a drastic overhaul if Sunderland's slump was to be arrested and the ship steadied.

Defence was another area where there was cause for concern. Reid had recruited and dumped countless defenders, and rarely settled on a fixed back four, with Michael Gray the only constant over the years. The close season of summer 2002 should have heralded further big spending but supporters were decidedly underwhelmed when the first signing was Phil Babb.

The ex-Liverpool centre half was part of the Scousers infamous 'Spice Boys' team of the mid 1990s, the prototype group of young, overpaid, underachieving players who went a long way towards sullying Liverpool's reputation as a great club. Babb had been playing for Sporting Lisbon, but the fact that he'd been voted the Portuguese defender of the year did little to enthuse Black Cats supporters who saw him as a cheap alternative to a real quality defender.

The only other new signing was Besiktas goalkeeper Thomas Myhre, who also arrived on a free transfer. By now, there were very few fans who were behind Peter

Reid, even though at one time, the majority of them would have echoed Bob Murray's thoughts that "if he goes so do I". Through a combination of spending big money on players who never played, stubbornly discarding stalwarts like Nicky Summerbee and Chris Makin for seemingly no good reason, while alienating internationals like Thomas Helmer, supporters had started to realise that this emperor really wasn't wearing any clothes.

Matters came to a head pre-season after a 2-1 defeat at Ghent in Belgium when a fan hurled beer over Reid as the manager headed for the dressing rooms. Earlier, deeply unpopular midfielder Kevin Kilbane, while being subjected to further abuse from fans, turned the tables and lobbed a V-sign in the direction of the supporters. Local fanzine *A Love Supreme* gauged the mood of the Wearside masses by launching two new designs to their wardrobe-bursting collection of designs. One read 'Reid Out', the other 'Reid In'. The former was easily the most popular.

It took another two pre-season losses and mounting fury before Reid purchased any more players. The club wallet had remained glued shut over the summer but was opened when Liverpool agreed to part company with their promising young right-back Stephen Wright for £3 million, a hefty wedge for a player who had made just 14 league appearances.

Reds fans didn't seem too concerned that Wright had gone. Days after the season had begun, another thrusting youngster was brought in to partner Wright on the right-hand flank, Leicester City's Matt Piper, for whom Reid forked out £3.5 million. Piper was said to be a quick skilful winger, but again, it was hard to tell as he had only made 16 league appearances.

The players showed their resolve from the traumas of pre-season and lost only one of their first four matches, picking up a win at Leeds United and a draw at home against Manchester United, the game in which United skipper Roy Keane blew his top and was sent off for elbowing Darren Williams. Quinn and Jason McAteer did their own little bit to pour fuel onto the fire and partisan fans across the nation were entertained immensely. But there were 10,000 empty seats at the first home match, against Everton. The Sunderland faithful were no longer feeling as though they were being entertained and were voting with their feet.

A day before the Manchester United game saw Sunderland splash the cash like they'd never done before on Tore Andre Flo from Glasgow Rangers and Ipswich Town's Marcus Stewart. August 2002 saw the introduction of the transfer window rule into the English Premiership and between the end of that month and the start of January, clubs would be forbidden from trading players.

The two forwards were brought in to bolster Sunderland's flimsy front line and the fans could no longer complain that the club weren't being pro-active in the transfer market.

Flo scored on his debut in that Manchester United game, but worryingly, the team saw the 6 ft 4 in forward as a new target man, another Quinn figure for them to lump long balls towards when there were no other valid options. Anyone who had watched Flo play for Rangers and Chelsea before that knew that the Norwegian international was in no way shape or form a target man. Although he was tall, he wasn't particularly strong, and winning headers was certainly not his forte, although he was deceptively skilful when the ball was played in to his feet.

Wright, Babb, Piper, Flo and Stewart all started in the home match with Fulham on September 14th, with Kevin Phillips out injured. It was one of the most depressing matches there had ever been at the Stadium of Light. Fulham comfortably collected the points, winning 3-0 and making Sunderland look like a pub team. The gulf in quality between the two sides was vast, but this was not Arsenal or Manchester United who had handed out a spanking – it was just Fulham.

The annual early-season trip to St James' Park came next. Whereas a couple of years before, Black Cats fans relished the short journey north, there was an air of foreboding this time. Thanks to some gruesome defending Sunderland were a goal down in under two minutes and 2-0 down at half-time. Newcastle cruised through the second half and should really have scored more. This was the one fixture where failing to give your all could not be accepted under any circumstances.

Reid still didn't have a clue who his best XI was, and speedy French boy David Bellion somehow earned a recall for the next home match with Aston Villa, along with Julio Arca, another player who looked to have been frozen out for no real reason. Reid's job was hanging by a thread now, but an unconvincing 1-0 win, with Arca setting up Bellion's goal, earned him a stay of execution. A 7-0 win at Cambridge followed in the Worthington Cup, although it was a men against boys affair and Reid fielded a full-strength team, evidently fearful of the consequences of a cup upset.

The axe finally fell on the jovial Scouser after a 3-1 Premiership defeat at Arsenal. Back then there was no real shame in losing at Highbury, but Sunderland capitulated from the first whistle, falling behind to two Kanu goals in the opening nine minutes.

The side's away form in 2002 had been horrendous, and time after time they were conceding early goals on their travels with nothing to offer in return. The new signings hadn't improved the team at all. The fact that so many of them arrived on the cusp of or even after the season had begun was laughable. Without a pre-season campaign for them all to blend in with each other, there was only going to be one outcome.

Reid had become an increasingly desperate figure in recent months. In his early days fans had sung 'Cheer Up Peter Reid' and had urged 'Reidy, Give Us A Wave' as he stalked the touchline, roaring profanity-riddled orders at his players. Towards the end he rarely left the dugout, like a wounded beast that was waiting to die. When he did come out, fans threw hard-earned beer at him. He had run out of ideas and the changes he made failed to work. While he had spent well at the lower end of the market, millions of pounds were wasted on foreign imports who never made the slightest impact on the Premiership. Rumours would later fly around about some of these deals, along with Reid's relationships with certain 'favoured' agents.

On the bright side, it was early in the season and Sunderland had won eight points from their first nine matches. A new face in the manager's seat could bring fresh impetus and help lift the expensively assembled squad up the table. Chairman Bob Murray called FA technical director Howard Wilkinson to ask his advice about who to approach for the job. It would be the stupidest phone call Murray would ever make.

CHAPTER ELEVEN

NEW YEAR'S RESOLUTION

If Roy Keane and Sunderland were going to get out of the quagmire that is the English League Championship, they would need to smarten up their act, develop a streak of ruthlessness and acquire some consistency. The side had shown they had the ability to grind out results but a killer instinct in front of goal was required if they were to collect enough points to get out of this league at the first attempt. One win in the four previous matches was most definitely not promotion form.

The new year was greeted with a visit to the Leicester City's Walkers Stadium. City were flirting with the relegation zone but would be no pushovers on their home patch. Chris Brown and Tobias Hysen were both given rare starts as Keane looked to freshen up the team after the defeat at home to Preston. The nightmarish toll of injuries that had ripped the defence apart meant that Dean Whitehead filled in at right-back with Ross Wallace playing at left-back.

Despite Sunderland's shortage of numbers, Leicester were second best from beginning to end, and although Sunderland controlled the play and created chance after chance, that nagging inability to find the back of the net meant it was tough going for the team and the 2,500 Black Cats fans who had once again hit the road with the team instead of staying in bed nursing their hangovers.

Sunderland's dominance was overwhelming, with 19 attempts on the Foxes' goal in the second half alone, but it took them until the 79th minute before they finally breached Leicester's defences, scoring twice in the last 12 minutes, both goals incorporating a slice of luck.

For the first, Whitehead broke free down the right before getting a cross in which Daryl Murphy met at the near post. As his shot crashed against the bar, it was looking like another near miss, but it bounced back into the path of Toby Hysen, who had gambled on a run into the box. With half of the goal wide open and unguarded, the Swede kept it simple and nodded the ball into the net from ten yards.

The Wearsiders finished the job off properly four minutes later – Murphy found himself in the clear but lost his concentration by checking to see if the linesman has raised an offside flag. Murphy kept his shot low, but it was poor and straight at the 'keeper. Again, Sunderland's fortune came from the rebound – the ball bounced out to David Connolly who made no mistake from the edge of the box.

As well as scoring his fifth goal for the club, Connolly collected himself a song that day too, a variation on the KC & The Sunshine Band classic *Give It Up*. Unlikely source material, but by now the clever Irish forward was becoming a firm fan favourite – his recent run of goals had clearly lifted his confidence and taken his all-round game up another notch.

The win lifted Sunderland into the top ten for the first time and although Roy Keane was happy with the improved performance, it wouldn't have changed his mind about the fact that reinforcements were urgently needed if the side were to have a realistic chance of pushing on and challenging for promotion. He reiterated that one or two players would be leaving in the coming days but that one or two would be arriving as well.

The first new face in through the door was 28-year-old Carlos Edwards, a Trinidad and Tobago international who signed from Luton Town for £1.5 million. Edwards had looked impressive down the right-hand side for the Hatters at the Stadium of Light a few weeks previously, and had played for his country in the 2006 World Cup alongside Dwight Yorke, who would no doubt have been quizzed by Roy Keane about the qualities and temperament of the new recruit. Prior to his spell with Luton, Edwards had spent five years at Wrexham, and begun his career with the magnificently-named Defence Force in Trinidad.

The second new signing was Jonny Evans, who arrived on loan from Manchester United the day after his 19th birthday. The youngster was said to be extremely highly-rated at Old Trafford and had just spent the first part of the season in Belgium with United's feeder club Royal Antwerp, where the side had remained unbeaten with Evans in their defence.

According to Evans, the deal between Sir Alex Ferguson and Keane had been negotiated through a series of text messages. Another United defender, Phil Bardsley was in the process of mulling over a loan move to Wearside and Keane had admitted he'd been in talks with the player.

There was a flurry of transfer activity in both directions in the first few days of 2007 as Keane said a permanent goodbye to those players who didn't figure in his plans. Robbie Elliott joined Leeds United while the loan moves of Liam Lawrence and the crocked Rory

Delap to Stoke City were made permanent. Marton Fulop also became a full-time Sunderland player, with Ben Alnwick heading to Spurs as part of the deal. Alnwick had paid a visit to Keane's office to voice his displeasure at being left out of the side, and after making that mistake, it was more or less a case of counting the days to his departure.

The FA Cup third round was next up for the Black Cats, with another match against Preston, the side who were becoming their nemesis for 2006–07. Jonny Evans made his full debut while Carlos Edwards had to make do with a place on the bench. Evans' proud unbeaten record for the season was about to be wiped out.

Sunderland started the game with the same sense of purpose that saw them collect three points at Leicester, a slightly more wired version of the display they'd put in against Preston at the Stadium of Light just over a week before. For the umpteenth time though, the end product was sorely lacking, and their domination produced nothing more than a couple of half-hearted goal attempts from Stephen Elliott and Liam Miller.

But, as David Nugent had done on Wearside, Brett Ormerod showed the value in having a striker who can carve a goal from just one isolated chance. As Ormerod ran on to a through ball which had bisected the Sunderland defence, Darren Ward came racing out of his box, sliding at the striker and the ball in an attempt to block his run. He failed and Ormerod had the fairly easy task of slotting the ball past Jonny Evans who had tracked back to cover the goal line.

With just over half an hour gone, there was still plenty of time left to get back into the match. Sunderland were unbowed by the goal and responded positively, continuing to press forward, but their luck ran out in the 37th minute when Liam Miller picked up his second yellow of the game after hacking down Nugent as the striker prepared to shoot from the edge of the area.

Keane's side continued to go at Preston – with the one-off nature of the game, they had nothing to lose – and they still looked confident that they could snatch an equaliser, even reverting to a 4-3-2 formation as the match drew towards its conclusion.

As they pushed forward they started to leave gaps at the back, which gave Jonny Evans a chance to get his hands dirty during his debut. The other debutant, Edwards, was brought on for his pace and to add to the side's width, but despite a great chance for Stephen Elliott three minutes from time, it wasn't enough and Sunderland's dreams of repeating the triumph of 1973 had disappeared before they'd begun. Not that a cup run was high on Roy Keane's agenda. He'd come into the job assuming that he'd get the side promoted at the first attempt and the FA Cup was a distraction that could wait for future seasons.

Preston manager Paul Simpson was complimentary about the Irishman and the team he was building, which he could afford to be when he'd just won. Simpson remarked that Keane was 'assembling a squad which is going to be the envy of managers in the Championship.' Keane found himself trying to find the positives in defeat again, saying, 'We deserved something but it was not to be and now we concentrate on the league.'

It would be a long time before he'd have to worry about defeat again.

There was a change in the striking department ahead of the next match at home against Ipswich, with two forwards leaving the club. Jon Stead had returned from his loan spell at Derby County but no permanent deal could be agreed, which meant that Lewin Nyatanga headed back to Pride Park, dashing his hopes that he'd be staying in the north east. Stead, the Poundstretcher Peter Crouch, looked to be in limbo until Neil Warnock came in with a deal which took the goal-shy striker to Sheffield United to aid them in their Premiership relegation battle.

Two goals in 40 appearances was a diabolical return for Stead, regardless of the quality of the team in which he was playing, and he would be remembered simply as an average player in a rotten side.

The other striker on the move was Chris Brown, who was signed by Norwich City. Brown's accuracy with an air pistol was arguably better than with a football, although his 11 goals in 69 matches was the stuff of dreams when compared to Stead's record.

Both players were deemed surplus to requirements as Keane had been successful in his protracted attempts to woo Irish under-21 prodigy Anthony Stokes back to the club that had rejected him following a trial in July 2006. Back then, Stokes was available only on loan, but now Arsenal had decided to cash in and the player opted for Sunderland when it looked as though he'd be headed to Celtic or Charlton. The 18-year-old came with an impressive pedigree and Sunderland fans assumed Stokes would instantly command a first team place and score the goals that would hoist the Black Cats up the table.

The young Irishman did get a starting place against Ipswich on January 13th, and with home debuts for Carlos Edwards and Jonny Evans, the Sunderland faithful got their first look at Roy Keane's new look line-up. Edwards and Stokes made an immediate impact, the winger feeding the ball down the line for Stokes to cross, the youngster sending it into the danger area between 'keeper and defenders.

No Ipswich player dared to get a touch on it and it

travelled to Connolly who was waiting at the back post to put the ball into the net.

Evans did his bit as well, clearing off the line to deny Ipswich an equaliser in what was far from a pretty match to watch, the blustery weather leading to a comeback for the small whirlwind of burger wrappers, plastic bags and general debris that swirl around the Stadium of Light pitch in such conditions.

Another three points and Sunderland were slowly advancing towards the business end of the league table, moving up to ninth place. If the new players could bed in quickly and the team could carry on as they had done in the last three games, the timing for a break into the top six could be perfect.

After a few false starts, Niall Quinn's magic carpet ride was definitely taking off now, and it was a staggering sight to witness more than 6,000 Sunderland fans packed into Hillsborough the following Saturday afternoon.

They were more privileged than they could possibly have known, as they would later get caught up in an attempt to break a world record and hijack a classic Beatles song, creating an anthem for the manager who looked to be finally steering the magic carpet towards the promised land.

As for the manager, he'd see his side collect three points, score four goals for the first time under his stewardship, while at the same time reducing him to a raging ball of fury.

Sunderland took the lead after 21 minutes with one of the best-worked goals of the season to date. Following a short corner, Sunderland played a series of confident passes across the edge of the Wednesday penalty area, culminating in a brilliant one-two between Dwight Yorke and Liam Miller. Miller's threaded return pass sent Yorke into space with just the Owls' 'keeper to beat, and he delicately lofted the ball over the 'keeper, putting Sunderland into a deserved lead.

With Yorke running the game from the centre of midfield, Sheffield Wednesday were unable to cope with Sunderland's pass-and-move game and the Black Cats got their second just before the break, putting them in a commanding position for the second half. Tobias Hysen sprinted into the six-yard area to convert Dean Whitehead's cross, the Swede's momentum carrying him into Stephen Elliott, who was also shaping up to put the ball in the back of the net.

At half-time, the veteran South Yorkshire heavy metal act Saxon made an audacious attempt to break the world air guitar record by trying to get the entire crowd to mime along to their new single. The response from Wednesday fans was muted at best – if your side were two goals down at home at half-time, would you put all of that pain and anguish to one side and pretend to play an imaginary guitar along to the sound of a gang of pensionable rockers for five minutes?

Exactly. Luckily for Saxon, most of the jubilant Sunderland fans were glad to join in with the stunt, and the day had a more significant musical flavour as it saw the debut of the mighty 'Hey Keano' song. Sung to the tune of The Beatles' *Hey Jude*, it would follow Sunderland and their manager around the country as the season wore on.

Wednesday upped their efforts following the break, but Sunderland were operating on a totally different level and there could have been no complaints when they went three goals in front and ended the game as a contest just before the hour.

Tobias Hysen advanced towards goal down the left-hand side, breaking into the Wednesday box before sliding a diagonal forward ball beyond the reach of the 'keeper to David Connolly, who although he looked offside, put the ball into the empty net.

Sunderland were home and hosed and started playing like it, taking their foot off the gas and relaxing when they should really have been containing the opposition while pressing for a fourth goal whenever the chance arose.

The visitors started getting sloppy and Wednesday sensed there could be a way back into the match. Deon Burton then scored what could only realistically be a consolation goal on 82 minutes when Darren Ward fumbled a free-kick from outside the box. The ball ricocheted straight back against Burton less than a yard from the goal line, and the ex-Derby striker couldn't have missed if he'd tried.

No need to worry, surely with just a few minutes remaining, Sunderland were still two goals clear. Five minutes later however, and their advantage had been reduced to just one goal, when Wade Small's shot from the right-hand side of Sunderland's penalty area flew past Ward.

To their credit, the Wearsiders didn't panic – seasoned supporters who had witnessed some truly gruesome performances over the years would probably have expected the capitulation to have been completed right at the death and a solitary point earned, or worse still, a 4-3 defeat. But, to their credit, the players kept their focus, and what should have been a cavernous win margin was confirmed as a comfortable one with a minute to go when Carlos Edwards tapped in his debut goal for the club after Crossley could only parry Daryl Murphy's cross-shot.

As 'Hey Keano' spread through the away end like a dose of the flu, inside the dressing room, the

Sunderland team were dealing with a different kind of headache. Their manager was not amused. In his mind, the players had no right to celebrate the victory as they hadn't finished the job off properly. Keane said, 'We got away with it. I was just disappointed generally with the performance.' When he was asked by radio commentator Simon Crabtree if any of the players had picked up injuries, the unhappy manager replied, 'Not yet.' What he would have been happy about was that only a lesser goal difference than Colchester kept his team out of the play-off zone.

Spurred on by the recent upturn in the team's fortunes on the pitch, but concerned by the slow increase in home attendance figures, Niall Quinn urged lapsed supporters to get back to the Stadium of Light and lift the team during the next phase of four matches, three of which were at home. Quinn had often waxed lyrical about the magical atmosphere which a full house at Sunderland can create.

The chairman said, 'Momentum is starting to gather pace and we need our fans to get behind the team, in numbers. We need to send out a statement of intent to teams coming to the Stadium of Light – the crowd made such a difference at Sheffield Wednesday and I'd like to see that replicated on home turf.'

The message fell on deaf ears. After a ten-day break during which the fourth round of the FA Cup was played, just 26,958 fans turned out on a frostbitten Tuesday evening to welcome Crystal Palace to the Stadium of Light. Palace came with a five man midfield intended to stifle Sunderland for the entire 90 minutes and it worked – the match ended goalless.

It was a game in which nothing happened. Nothing whatsoever. It wasn't even a bad game, it was just... dull. In fact, the most exciting part of the evening was the fact that referee's name was Trevor Kettle. That's how dreary it all was.

Better was expected the following Saturday with another home game, against Coventry City. In the interim period after Sheffield Wednesday, the manager stocked up further on new players. Firstly, in the wake of his failed attempt to borrow Phil Bardsley (the player chose Aston Villa instead,) Keane persuaded Sir Alex Ferguson to loan him Manchester United's young right-back Danny Simpson.

The method of communication used on this occasion is not known. It may have been text message again, or it could have been email, MySpace messaging or even a mssage in a bottle. However it happened, the deal was done, and Simpson, who had also played for Royal Antwerp with Jonny Evans, was a Sunderland player until the end of the season.

A further addition to the squad was made, in the hulking shape of Coventry City's Stern John, who had scored a brilliant goal against the Black Cats on the opening day of the season. The fact that Sunderland paid Coventry around £300,000 for John – their top scorer – and had received twice that amount from them for fifth-rate plank Kevin Kyle (three goals in 33 games in his first season for the Sky Blues) was a source of much amusement, even if Stern John, another Trinidad and Tobago international, turned out not to be that much better.

The most surprising deal was the sale of former captain Steven Caldwell to Burnley for £400,000, a deal completed with just nine minutes of the transfer window remaining.

Keane intimated that he had been unhappy with Caldwell's recurring visits to the treatment room as well as the ongoing discussions with his agent over an extension to his contract. That was that – Caldwell was gone.

John made his debut against his old side within days of arriving at Sunderland, replacing the injured David Connolly. Jonny Evans and Liam Miller also both missed out with injuries, although in the end the strength in depth the side now had meant that they weren't missed a great deal. Daryl Murphy returned in place of Anthony Stokes and Ross Wallace swapped his place on the bench with Tobias Hysen.

Coventry approached the match with a similar mentality to that of Crystal Palace, to suffocate Sunderland and play out a draw. True, the Midlanders were a little more lively and mischievous than Palace, and looked to counter-attack whenever they got the chance. Their plan was scuppered after just 19 minutes.

Sunderland won a free-kick about 35 yards from goal on the right-hand touchline. Ross Wallace spun it into the danger area at the back post with his left foot, a difficult ball to defend against. It fell to Varga at the bye-line who hooked it high, back toward the middle of the goal where Dwight Yorke arrived, spring-heeled, heading the ball beyond the 'keeper from four yards out.

Coventry refused to alter their game plan, sticking to it in the hope that it would eventually pay off and they'd be able to steal an equaliser. The plan almost worked, and Darren Ward had to be at his very best to keep a clean sheet. Sunderland's ongoing search for a penalty continued – Coventry was the 60th match since they'd had one. Keane spoke about the spot-kick famine afterwards, saying, 'I've seen the Carlos Edwards penalty incident near the end again on video and it's not even funny anymore.'

As well as being felled in the box, Edwards gave Black

Cats fans the first glimpse of his capabilities when given the ball, a yard of space, and a sight on goal. His 25-yard right-footed blast got a deflection off a Coventry defender which made it impossible to save, but Edwards' second Sunderland goal would be consigned to the also-ran pile when it came to choosing his best at the end of the season.

That goal came after 84 minutes and wrapped up Sunderland's third win in four games, lifting them back up to seventh place. What was notable once again was the excellent display by Nyron Nosworthy, playing at centre half again rather than his preferred right-back role. In the 18 months since he'd signed from Gillingham, Nosworthy had been a combination of class clown and cult hero. Infectiously enthusiastic, his biggest letdown was his unusual methods with the ball at his feet. It's hard to forget him conceding a corner from the halfway line at Middlesbrough in 2005 when there wasn't another player within ten yards of him, but with his combination of strength and pace now being applied to the centre-back role, maybe there was hope for him yet. Playing in a team that had learned how to win couldn't hurt.

CHAPTER TWELVE

THE CATS GET
THE CREAM

AS FEBRUARY 2007 rolled around and the weather worsened, the outlook at Sunderland was brighter than it had been in years. Under the new ownership of Niall Quinn's Drumaville consortium, the financial worries that had blighted the club's progress for half a decade were gone. On the football side, Roy Keane was slowly proving that the challenge of getting the club out of the Championship at the first attempt might just be one to which he could rise.

The squad was taking shape with the addition of defenders Jonny Evans and Danny Simpson from Manchester United, while the team's attack looked much more purposeful as Carlos Edwards and Anthony Stokes settled in. Jonny Evans in particular had hit the ground running, and looked as though he'd been a part of the team for years, displaying the innate positional sense and assured style of a player ten years his senior. The Old Trafford connection infiltrated Keane's support team too – Neil Bailey became first team coach, a reprise of his role at Manchester United's academy.

In the wake of the Coventry win, Sunderland were sitting in seventh place, just outside the play-off zone, but up at the top on current form. Looming large were consecutive games against Birmingham, Derby and West Brom, the three sides who (along with Preston) were battling over the two automatic promotion spots at that time. Beat Plymouth Argyle and Southend and Sunderland would go into that run of three matches knowing that everything was to play for. Stumble in those next two games however, and a top two spot would probably be out of reach.

Down at Plymouth, Marton Fulop had another chance to claim the goalkeeping jersey after a hamstring strain ruled out Darren Ward, and the Hungarian had to make a couple of vital early saves as both sides came close to taking the lead, with nothing to separate them at the end of an open first half. On one occasion when Fulop was beaten, Carlos Edwards had got back and cleared off the line.

Roy Keane had probably expected more from his on-form side and the way Sunderland grasped the nettle after the interval suggested that one or two strong words had been uttered during the break. The visitors took the game to Argyle from the restart and were beginning to dominate when Keane made a substitution on 66 minutes that would turn the game on its head.

Anthony Stokes was introduced from the bench and put on the left wing in place of Toby Hysen. Within three minutes Stokes showed why Keane had doggedly pursued his signature, hitting an angled shot from 25 yards out on the left, which, while bouncing twice on its way, was still too much for Plymouth's 'keeper to deal with. Sunderland were in front and, thanks to the Manchester United boys in defence, were becoming the kind of team that didn't easily give leads up.

Two minutes later, and Sunderland wrapped it up. A ball hooked out of Sunderland's defence reached Stern

John who brilliantly worked his marker and flicked it on into the path of David Connolly. The striker gave himself a couple of yards head start against the Plymouth defender before selling the 'keeper a dummy, taking it around him and stroking it into the net. Two-nil to Sunderland and the mistakes made at Sheffield Wednesday were unlikely to be repeated. Now only goal difference was keeping the Wearsiders out of the top six.

An era came to an end at the club with the news that Bobby Saxton would be leaving. Peter Reid's gruff former number two came to the rescue of Niall Quinn when the chairman briefly became the manager, but with Roy Keane's desire to bring in his own people, there was no longer any room for Saxton, who departed along with the club's chief scout Bob Shaw. Shaw's role would be filled by Mick Brown, the former chief scout at Manchester United, who had also been working for England boss Steve McClaren but would now turn his attentions to bringing Sunderland's scouting system up among the best in the country.

It was further evidence that Keane was looking to transform the club from top to bottom and leave no stone unturned in his quest for perfection. The ethos followed on directly from his attitude as a player, and echoed the dictatorial style of management carried out so effectively by his mentors Brian Clough and Sir Alex Ferguson. It's unlikely that there'll be a director of football employed at Sunderland AFC while Roy Keane is there.

Although they were second from bottom of the league, Southend had won four of their last six matches and were up at the top of the form table with the Black Cats. 'Bucket & Spade FC,' as their fans' flag read, made the long trek to the Stadium of Light on February 17th as the final third of the season kicked in. Ominously for the rest of the clubs chasing promotion, it was the day when Sunderland made it into the top six for the first time.

It had been less than six months since the two sides had last met, back on that infamous day at the seaside when Sunderland got buried up to their necks and had sand kicked in their faces in that woeful 3-1 defeat at Roots Hall. What was noteworthy was that only Dean Whitehead had survived from the starting XI of that day in August – the Keane machine had ruthlessly phased out those players who weren't up to the job of getting Sunderland promoted.

The manager kept an unchanged back five, with Fulop retaining his place between the sticks. The defence consisted of Danny Simpson and Danny Collins at right and left-back, with Nyron Nosworthy and Jonny Evans playing in the centre. Keane would settle on this back four for the rest of the season, with only one change made between the middle of February and the final day at Luton.

Southend were comprehensively beaten 4-0 at the Stadium of Light, with two goals at either end of the match, a win which took Sunderland to within five points of an automatic promotion spot.

The home side took the lead in the fourth minute when Edwards aggressively robbed the left-back and raced towards the bye-line and into the box, squaring a perfect low ball beyond the 'keeper's reach for David Connolly to convert simply and efficiently. It was Connolly's eighth goal in his last 11 games, a run of form that had come at the perfect moment to boost Sunderland's season.

Stern John should have scored his first Sunderland goal and made it 2-0 a few minutes later. But his header bounced off the inside of the post, and failed to cross the line. There was no undue need to worry – the second goal came soon after on 13 minutes. Tobias Hysen superbly took down a pass from Connolly on the left-hand side before advancing into the penalty area, nicking it round his defender and comfortably slotting the ball to the 'keeper's left and into the corner of the net.

The Wearsiders were firmly in control of the game from then on, with any Southend threat snuffed out by the Wearsiders' back line, Jonny Evans in particular looking a class above the level of football being played. The only question that was posed was when, rather than if, Sunderland would get the third goal that would seal their third straight win. Dean Whitehead got down the right only to see his shot bounce back off the post – it rebounded to Stern John, who would never score an easier goal, tapping it into an empty net, getting himself off the mark as a Sunderland player and putting the home side three goals to the good.

John got his second a couple of minutes later, taking full advantage of what was now a battered and bewildered opposition defence. A cross from the right evaded the entire Southend back line, straight to John, who was standing on the edge of the six-yard box like someone hanging around for a bus to arrive. A ball came instead, and he caught it on the half-volley, sending it straight past the Southend 'keeper.

Sunderland made that important jump into the play-off zone for the first time, but their scintillating run of form meant that there was no time for celebration. Their only goal now was an automatic promotion spot – Roy Keane would deem anything else as failure, and the next three games would see just how resolute the manager's new team really were.

First up was St Andrews and Birmingham City, then in second-place and looking to take all three points to edge nearer to league leaders Derby County. The Brummies were sitting three points behind Derby with two games in hand and needed to win to gain back some of that lost ground. But Sunderland were only four points behind Birmingham and desperate to close the gap. Keane's men took the game to the Blues from the off, looking more like the home side and dominating possession. Anthony Stokes made the most of his first start in four matches, in an unfamiliar left wing role, but he was quick and direct without being selfish, looking to set up the strikers and linking up particularly well with David Connolly.

Despite their majority share of the possession, Sunderland weren't threatening Colin Doyle's goal, or at least they weren't until Carlos Edwards picked up the ball midway in Birmingham's half and set off, galloping infield and towards the penalty area with only one thought in his mind. The Birmingham players clearly weren't on the same wavelength as the winger as they stood off him, and Edwards' 20 yard shot into the top corner showed that his left foot could be just as potent as his right. Twenty-seven minutes gone and Sunderland were in the lead again.

The Black Cats hadn't taken the lead in a match and not gone on to win it for more than three months – since the home game with Southampton. As the match drew ever nearer to its end it was looking as though another three points were theirs and the promotion race was about to be blown wide open. Enter a player who had a bit of previous history with Sunderland.

Back in January 2006, a former non-league striker with a vaguely superstar name put Sunderland out of the FA Cup when the club were at their lowest ebb. His name was DJ Campbell and then he was a Brentford player. He had since moved to Birmingham and the Curse of Campbell struck again with virtually the last kick of the game. As Birmingham increased the pressure on the Sunderland goalmouth, they won a corner which was cleared but immediately driven back into the box, pinging around before Campbell got a sufficient touch on it to put it into the net. A point gained? No, two lost.

But Keane was sanguine about it all, or at least he was in public 'I'm OK with the result, we take the positives out of it and now we look forward to another big game on Saturday,' he said. 'It was an open game, an entertaining game. If we'd managed to get that second goal I'm sure we'd have gone on to win it. But we had a go and I hope our fans enjoyed it.' The manager also stated that he'd expect his team to go unbeaten for the twelve games that remained, which is probably what would be needed if they were to make it into the top two.

The Saturday game he referred to was a bigger test again, at home against league leaders Derby County, and the Sunderland manager wasn't shy when it came to talking up his side's chances either. 'The next few months will sort out the men from the boys and I've got a few men in my dressing room, so I'm quite relaxed about it,' Keane said, adding, 'We're ready for it tomorrow.'

But it seemed that Derby's manager, Billy Davies, possibly wasn't ready for it. Interviewed on television ahead of the game, he appeared to be haunted and unsure, as if he knew that Sunderland catching up with Derby was inevitable. He shouldn't have been worried, as Derby's rise up the table had been even more meteoric than Sunderland's. When Roy Keane arrived and took the points away from Pride Park in early September, the result pushed Derby into the bottom three. Davies had rallied his team and they'd ground out wins against most of the teams in the league since then.

But their manager seemed spooked when talking to Sky Sports News, as though he knew what was coming next. Psychologically, Sunderland were as good as a goal up before the first turnstile at the Stadium of Light had opened. The crowds going through those turnstiles were getting bigger too, with over 33,000 to see the 4-0 win over Southend, and the gate increased to 36,049 with the arrival of Derby.

The source of the Black Cats' first goal was a thing of wonderment and surprise. Sixty-three matches since the last one, a 15 month drought, and Sunderland had the ball placed on that little white spot twelve yards front and centre from the goal-line. Connolly, whose shirt had been yanked at in the box, stepped up to take the elusive penalty and send the 'keeper the wrong way.

The home side's performance in the first half was superb. Pitted against the leaders of the pack, Sunderland had no time for deference, seeing Derby as just another obstacle standing between them and promotion. Search and destroy. There were more chances to score and they should have taken them, but Sunderland had been either wasteful or not creative enough all season and it was happening again.

They paid for it in the second half. Derby came out a different side, probably with a reminder that they were top of the league still ringing in their ears. The Rams' teenage sensation, Giles Barnes, was unleashed on the match and added some unpredictability into the play and sure enough, it was Barnes who orchestrated and scored the equaliser.

He got hold of the ball on the edge of Sunderland's penalty area, improvising a breathtaking bit of skill where he stepped on the ball and spun 360 degrees, leaving Danny Collins for dead and creating enough space for himself to fire a close-range shot past Ward. If Ronaldinho or Messi had scored it, footage of it would have been all over the world within hours. A goal apiece with half an hour to go.

As at Birmingham, the game crept towards its conclusion – a point would suit Derby more than it would Sunderland, and it was that fact that led the home side's charge, firing their resolve to keep their foot down that little bit longer, and go after the winner.

With three minutes of injury time played and the match still alive, Grant Leadbitter had the ball wide on the left, level with the Derby penalty box. After shifting the ball into a yard of space, he sent in a cross which found Liam Miller eight yards out in the centre of the penalty area. Miller got a glancing header on the ball, giving it just enough upward trajectory to make it fly above the helpless dive of goalkeeper Stephen Bywater.

This was it. That one second, that one delicate headed flick, the right place at the right time, the goal would act as a catalyst for everything else that Sunderland would have coming to them during the rest of the season.

That header stands as a huge turning point in the recent history of the football club. It was the moment when the jaded masses were awoken and fell in love with all things Sunderland again. Those fans had been wounded back when it all fell apart under Peter Reid after Bob Murray had sworn to them that the club would never be relegated again. They didn't trust Murray, but they trusted Reid and so they believed it all. In the end it turned out that Murray had been dewy-eyed with admiration for the Scouser's achievements. Couple that with the bright, shiny new stadium the chairman had built and all perspective went flying out of the expensive tinted windows.

The club's health never fully recovered from that 19 point season of 2002–03, back when the average attendance was a shade under 40,000. Unbelievable – but then, many of them were season ticket holders who'd felt obliged to go to the matches. Two years later, when Mick McCarthy took the club back up again as champions, the average gate was somewhere in the region of 28,000. A quarter of the core support had gone and not even another Championship title could bring them back.

The team performed heroically in 2004–05, winning 29 of their 46 games. But there was a haunted feeling about it all, as though something was missing. Sunderland had won it and done it better a few years ago, and a hangover was still in place. That McCarthy had made it happen on the cheap was incredible but they should never again have had to dig their way out of that league. Promises had been made and been broken. The relationship between the club and its supporters had been tainted and it wasn't going to be rectified overnight.

The broken-hearted were at first wary of Keane. Even of Quinn, and his talk of restoring the pride. But slowly and surely, they were coming back and when Liam Miller's winner against Derby crossed the line and fell into the back of the net, it both brought back the love and took the roof off the place.

Miller raced towards the north east corner flag, where a troop of adrenalin-fuelled maniacs poured out of the stand towards him. Those that remained in or somewhere near their seats were hugging strangers, season ticket holders were kissing their match-day neighbours, people with whom they were usually only on nodding terms. As the man had promised, it was like being on a magic carpet ride.

There was no time for Derby to do anything in response. With hindsight, they were knocked out right then. Everything they'd achieved in the months after Sunderland had done them 3-1 at Pride Park was all they had left to hold on to. They were in a slump that would eventually knock them out of the top two. Six wins in the last 14 games isn't the stuff of champions, but it would be all that the Rams were capable of mustering after they left the north east with nothing.

For Sunderland, there were 11 games remaining and they were now just three points away from that sacred automatic promotion spot.

If Miller's head hadn't connected perfectly with that cross from Leadbitter, they would have ended the game six behind Derby and dropped to ninth in the league. But Miller judged and executed it to perfection and now they were just three points behind Derby, in fourth place. Promotion, the Championship trophy, it was all now well within sight, and what better time to have a crack at West Bromwich Albion, the team directly above them.

In the interim, Roy Keane received the Manager of the Month prize for February, doubtless not the last award of his managerial career. But Keane knows a thing or two about winning, and was quick to point out that nothing of note is won in February, saying, 'There's no point getting an award halfway through the season. It kind of irritates me and it did when I was a player. The award will probably go in the garage – I'm focusing on our match at West Brom.'

Sunderland started March as if Keane would have to clutter up his garage with another award. The third part of what could have been a hellish trilogy of matches was looming and Sunderland were hungry for it, eager to get in among the promotion pack for the final ten games.

The supporters were looking ahead to future conquests. More than two and a half thousand of them would be travelling to The Hawthorns, and Sunderland had negotiated a whopping 8,000 tickets for the upcoming trip to Barnsley. A long, snaking queue formed at the Stadium of Light for Barnsley tickets, which pleased Niall Quinn greatly when he arrived at the ground that morning. The chairman said, 'It's incredible. Seeing the fans gave me a great feeling driving into work. I even took a couple of pictures on my phone and sent them to people.'

Now on a run of nine wins and two draws in their last 11 games, Sunderland were starting to look as though Roy Keane's view that they could go the rest of the season without defeat might in fact come true. Keane had kept it simple for the players – knowing that the team's defence was finally settled and running smoothly, in no small part thanks to the combination of Nosworthy and Evans in the middle, he told the players that if they scored twice or more in each of their remaining games, they would be promoted.

They did indeed get their two goals and the three points at The Hawthorns, but it was never easy. West Brom had the better of the first quarter of the match, and it was all Sunderland could do to keep out their opponents. Then, with their first real attack, the Wearsiders took the lead. Danny Simpson went on a run infield from the right touchline before playing the ball forward. His pass reached Stern John, who guided it deftly into the path of Dwight Yorke, who had broken from midfield. The veteran's first time shot was impeccable, sweeping the ball along the ground, past the 'keeper's left hand to leave it nestling in the bottom corner of the net.

The goal gave Sunderland the confidence to take the game to the home side, and helpfully, West Brom seemed affected by Yorke's sucker punch, allowing Sunderland to take control. There were no further goals in the first half, but the 2,600 Sunderland fans got their reward after less than five minutes of the second half.

The goal that doubled their lead started with a high corner kick from Dean Whitehead on the left which sailed to the back post where two Sunderland players were inexplicably unmarked. This was too easy – Stern John leapt and headed the ball back across goal just as the 'keeper arrived to challenge for it. Two-nil and the game was Sunderland's for the taking.

West Brom's manager Tony Mowbray made a triple substitution, which only served to highlight his panic. Kevin Phillips was one of the players who made way – possibly the last time Sunderland fans would ever see their former idol in the flesh. The changes revitalised West Brom, and Darren Carter made it interesting again with a blinding strike from outside the box that flew across Darren Ward and into the net.

The Baggies could sense an equaliser was there to be had and increased the pressure on Sunderland, but Evans and Nosworthy were in tremendous form, keeping out everything chucked at them. The home team's hopes of equalising vanished with a couple of minutes remaining when Paul Robinson was sent off after pulling back Liam Miller as he raced through in an attempt to get Sunderland's third.

Another win, and a sequence of ten wins and two draws in their last dozen games: 32 points out of a possible 36. The points gained were not enough for them to leapfrog West Brom, but they drew level on goal difference. Birmingham and Derby had both won as well, and so promotion didn't really seem any closer than it had done at 2.59pm that afternoon.

Sunderland fans at The Hawthorns had unfurled a Trinidad and Tobago flag on the day Dwight Yorke and Stern John scored the goals that won those three points at The Hawthorns and John later said that the sight of it gave him goosebumps. But the third T&T international on display didn't have such a good day – Carlos Edwards suffered a damaged shoulder and early reports suggested he could be out for the remainder of the season.

It might have paid Tony Mowbray had he taken a leaf out the Caribbean book and reacted to his side's defeat with a relaxed shrug of the shoulders. Instead, Mowbray launched into a weird, deluded rant against the team that had won the match, saying 'We're a better footballing side. We score more goals because of the way we play and we'll win more matches than them. What's more, we're still above them.'

Time would tell, but Sunderland's fans had got their point across during the match, singing 'And now you're gonna believe us, we're gonna win the league.' Time would tell.

CHAPTER THIRTEEN

A DECADE OF LIGHT
CHEAP AND NASTY

AT THE TURN of the millennium it was hard to imagine a Sunderland AFC without Peter Reid. In five years he had taken a side on the brink of dropping into the English league's third tier, got them promoted, relegated and then promoted again, before putting together a team that was knocking on the door of the UEFA Cup. All of this coincided with the move to a brand new purpose-built home within the confines of the city. To fans of a club like Sunderland, who had been starved of any meaningful success for six decades (two FA Cup wins aside,) the progress was the stuff of dreams. Eighteen months after sitting in second place in the Premiership, it had become a living nightmare.

Reid's shadow loomed large over every aspect of the club as success piled up and the Wearsiders looked primed to become a permanent fixture in the top flight. Sunderland's chairman Bob Murray, the dour kitchen and bathroom magnate, thanked his lucky stars that he'd finally found a manager who could make a real go of the Sunderland job as opposed to the string of losers and chancers he'd employed in the past.

But Reid only had one real strategy and it revolved

around the use of Niall Quinn as a target man. Once Quinn's powers began to diminish, Reid was charged with either replacing him with a like-minded player or adapting to a new game plan. He could do neither, and as he froze out useful, popular players while replacing them with inferior versions, Sunderland's descent was inevitable. Reid was sacked nine games into the 2002–03 season, after spending more than £20 million during his last year in charge. Neither good timing nor sound business sense by Murray.

With the era of Peter Reid over, Murray made a call to Howard Wilkinson, then the FA technical director, with the idea of picking Wilkinson's brains as to a potential successor to Reid. Wilkinson put forward just one name – his own. This was good enough for Murray; after all, who knew Wilko's strengths better than the man himself?

The appointment was met with disbelief and derision among the wider footballing community. Wilkinson was a man with a dry sense of humour, the sort which doesn't translate well into print and was largely seen as a figure to be ridiculed. He didn't do himself any favours during his time at Sunderland with quotes like 'Our squad looks good on paper. But paper teams win paper cups,' and (on the team's inability to pick up points) 'It's like trying to push custard up a hill with your finger'.

As his right-hand man and managerial protégé, Wilkinson ransacked Stoke City for their promising manager Steve Cotterill. A serious young man with a West Country burr and a sackful of coaching badges, Cotterill's role appeared to be prowling the touchline in a pair of shorts slightly too small for him while scribbling furiously on a note pad. What was he writing? His memoirs? A shopping list? Experimental poetry? Whatever it was, it didn't help much.

The Howard and Steve show started fairly promisingly

– after losing 1-0 at home against West Ham, Sunderland were unbeaten in their next five matches, four of which were away from home. The run culminated in a hugely entertaining 0-0 draw at Liverpool, where Sunderland seemed to deploy a 1-10 formation. The Black Cats failed to create a single chance in the whole of the match, but 'keeper Jurgen Macho had the game of his life, keeping out the Reds and their 24 shots, ten of which were on target. It helped fans to warm to the new manager – whatever the method, a point at Anfield was a point at Anfield.

The players were becoming fitter and more regimented, with two training sessions per day, and for a while, it looked as though Howard's way might the right way for Sunderland. But after the rearguard action at Anfield, Sunderland lost their next four on the trot, without scoring a single goal. A win at the Stadium of Light in the return match against the Scouse reds brought some temporary relief, but the defeats soon started to mount up again, with three 2-1 reversals in the space of a week particularly hard to bear.

Players were continuing to disappear from the team with inadequate replacements taking their place. Niall Quinn announced his inevitable retirement shortly after Wilkinson took over, and first-choice centre-half Emerson Thome suddenly disappeared from the team after his 49th league and FA Cup appearance. It was suggested that a 50th appearance would trigger a further payment to Chelsea, something which the club's finances couldn't stretch to. It seemed that Reid had bled Sunderland dry in the summer and left them with a squad of players who were wholly incapable of staying in the top flight. What's more, Murray had let him do it.

Howard Wilkinson's mission impossible went from bad to worse into 2003. Another rearguard action at Old Trafford almost paid off but ended in a 2-1 defeat, and free of the psychological shackles of the league, the team went on a mini-FA Cup run, reaching the fifth round. But one game will live forever in the tainted minds of those who witnessed it, a shambolic debacle of a match at the Stadium of Light where reality and reason seemingly failed to bother turning up.

The visitors were Charlton Athletic, and between 3.24pm and 3.31pm on the afternoon of February 1st 2003, Sunderland self-destructed in as spectacular a fashion as any team has done before or since. More than 36,000 horrified fans watched through their fingers as Sunderland went 3-0 down in those seven minutes, with every one of them an own goal – the first from defender Stephen Wright and the other two from young striker Michael Proctor. In that short space of time, Proctor matched the two goals he'd scored at the right end earlier in the season, and it would be nigh-on 11 months before he'd hit the back of the net in the league again.

Distressed fans tried to get out of the stadium after the third goal went in but stewards told them it would be more than their jobs were worth to let them out. A similar attempt by what were technically prisoners to get the bars inside the ground to open early, and allow them to drown their sorrows, also failed. Those who stayed for the second half saw the humour in the situation and a Mexican wave broke out around the ground, with bemused Charlton fans happy to join in.

When the whole of your home support is laughing in the face of such horror, it's time to go, and Wilkinson didn't last much longer. It was five more games to be precise, with the final four all ending in defeat. With just nine games left in the season, Sunderland had accumulated a measly 19 points and relegation was a certainty. Bob Murray realised that he'd made a colossal mistake and that appointing Peter Reid, a manager who actually won things, had just been a blip among the long list of underachieving goons Murray had allowed to run riot with the hearts and souls of Sunderland fans for two decades.

If it weren't for the fact that Bob Murray had finally sanctioned vast amounts of cash to be spent on the team before sacking the man who he'd permitted to spend it, it might be funny. If it weren't for the fact that said team looked like a confused set of individuals who'd only been introduced to each other 20 minutes before the kick-off, it might be funny. If it weren't for the fact that said individuals were putting in such dire performances that relegation was all but inevitable, it might be funny.

The man charged with trying to salvage something from this wreck of a season was Mick McCarthy. The former Republic of Ireland boss was out of work so there'd be no nasty compensation for skint Sunderland to have to cough up. McCarthy was the initial favourite to get the job after Reid was fired, but his chance came now, and he had nine games to assess what he'd have to work with in the second tier a few months later.

The appointment was popular with the majority of fans but some supporters were wary. After all, the man was caught out during a TV interview after Ireland lost to Spain in the 2002 World Cup. McCarthy hadn't realised that the Spanish had played most of extra time with only ten men, having used all their subs and lost another player to injury. Surely an international manager should spot something as obvious as a player missing from the opposing team? Then there was the baggage from the Roy Keane fall-out. Was McCarthy a committed professional or did he lack the thorough eye for detail and preparation that Keane espoused? Was he a convenient choice – desperate to get back into management and happy to take a job that nobody else in their right mind would go within a mile of?

A straight-talking, no-nonsense Yorkshireman with Irish

heritage McCarthy was in a win–win situation. String a few results together and it'd be 'if only he'd got the job sooner.' Lose the majority of the remaining games and his line would be 'not my fault guv'nor – they're not my players.'

He lost the lot. All nine of them, a worse record than either Reid or Wilkinson's for that season. His team conceded 19 goals and scored just twice, finishing the season on 19 points, the worst Premiership points total of any club to date. Two years prior, Sunderland had finished seventh, had more than 40,000 fans attending every home match and had ample amounts of cash to invest in new players. To this day, it beggars belief how they could have so quickly gone from one extreme to the other.

The club's response to relegation was both swift and brutal. Staff were laid off, genuine hard-working folk in administrative positions at the club, or people who worked in the canteen. The sort of people who weren't earning hundreds of thousands of pounds for not pulling their weight on the football field. The players wearing the red and white shirts and those who led them were to blame for it all, but their lives wouldn't be affected all that much – the players would be sold to another club, pocket another hefty signing-on fee and carry on living their charmed lives. The chairman wasn't prepared to bail out the club with any of his vast personal fortune so things steadily got worse.

The scales fell from the eyes of Sunderland fans when it emerged that Kevin Phillips had submitted numerous transfer requests that had been turned down, and when the player admitted that he hadn't felt motivated in his final season on Wearside, Super Kev instantly stopped being One Of Us – a lad who came from the non-league into football's land of milk and honey and wound up winning Europe's Golden Boot. He became One Of Them

– another half-arsed pro footballer, riding the gravy train while not giving a damn that he was plying his trade in front of adoring fans in one of the economic black holes of Britain, fans who really had to dig deep to carry on watching a club where admission had gone from a fiver to thirty quid a shot in a few years.

A fire sale took place, and anyone who had any worth at all was on their way out, almost all of them for a knock-down price. Phillips, Sorensen, McCann, Craddock, Thome, Kilbane, the heart of a side that had almost made it into Europe. Had Quinn been carrying the lot of them while he'd still been able? Other lesser names were sold too; Flo, Reyna, Laslandes all went, while one of the few positives that came from it all was that Sunderland received £2 million for the quick but utterly useless David Bellion.

Mick McCarthy had to start from scratch and build a new side of grafters with as much skill as he could possibly round up. The transfer budget was zero as Bob Murray declared that transfer fees were a thing of the past. Irish internationals Gary Breen and Colin Healy were produced out of thin air. Tommy Smith came from Watford on a free and was joined by Jeff Whitley, ex-Manchester City and as whole-hearted as he was limited.

Players who weren't sold went on to form the backbone of the new-look side. Julio Arca could probably have earned himself a move to another Premiership club but the Argentine left-winger felt that he wanted to repay the Sunderland fans for their loyalty. Or perhaps his wages weren't excessive enough to warrant getting rid of him. Others like Joachim Bjorklund and Stephen Wright stuck around to try and get the club back up at the first time of asking. Jason McAteer was still there, but for someone who had been a Liverpool first-teamer, his contribution was negligible.

The real star of that hotchpotch of a side was Marcus

Stewart. Like David Connolly in 2006–07, Stewart's off the ball play was too confusing for defenders at this lower level, and coupled with his eye for goal, he started to shine for the first time since arriving on Wearside in a blaze of glory with the ineffective Tore Andre Flo.

Sunderland stuttered through the early months of the season, with fans enduring a six-match run without a win ahead of the Christmas period. It was only in the New Year that the team started to gel, and a sequence of matches where the team lost only once in a dozen games helped lift them into play-off reckoning.

The streak of form coincided with a run in the FA Cup, and Tommy Smith's winner in a 1-0 defeat of Sheffield United at the Stadium of Light sent Sunderland into their first FA Cup semi-final since 1992. Thoughts of 1973 came rushing to the foreground too – amazingly, Sunderland's three most recent appearances in the last four of the competition occurred when the Wearsiders were in the second tier of the league.

But even though a place in a cup semi-final was on offer, only 37,115 fans turned up against Sheffield United. The sense that fans had been betrayed by the club still lingered and many vowed not to return until Bob Murray had departed. That would still be some way away. Cup fever started to take hold when the draw revealed that Sunderland had avoided Manchester United and Arsenal and that only fellow Division One side Millwall stood between the Black Cats and a trip to Cardiff.

On the day, Sunderland should have won the match and got to the final but they didn't perform. Millwall took the lead in the first half from Tim Cahill, and although the Wearsiders battled through an even-handed match, McCarthy didn't do enough to take the game to the opposition, bringing on Stewart to add some more thrust to the attack, but removing Kyle who would still have posed an aerial threat if Stewart could have been accommodated behind the front two. In a win-or-bust situation, what was there to lose? Jason McAteer was sent off in the 85th minute and a 1-0 defeat was a severely disappointing outcome.

The team didn't dwell on it and comfortably gained a place in the play-offs without ever really troubling the top two. Crystal Palace would be their opponents in the semi-final, and the season would fizzle out right at the last as the South Londoners made it through to the final.

McCarthy's judgment in big-game situations was questioned again against Palace. Sunderland had lost the first leg 3-2 at Selhurst Park, but made up for it by going 2-0 up in the first half of the return at the Stadium of Light. Again a 34,536 crowd was a poor showing given the magnitude of the occasion. Palace came at Sunderland in the second half as they tried to get the goal that would lead to extra time but it wouldn't fall for them and Sunderland defended stoutly. It looked to be all over when Palace's Julian Gray was sent off with five minutes remaining. With their opponents down to ten men and needing a goal, all the home side had to do was keep the ball, run down the clock, get it in the corners, just get the job done.

Instead, they conceded possession and then conceded a corner. There was almost certainly a foul on Poom when Derry's corner came in but it wasn't given and the ball ended up in the back of the net courtesy of Darren Powell. Extra time was played out with Sunderland unable to use their numerical advantage to grab a winner; Palace would settle for the lottery of the penalty shoot-out.

Penalties and play-offs don't sit right with Sunderland – it was no big surprise when Palace went through late, late into the May night. The culprit was Jeff Whitley, who, for reasons that may never be known, decided to do a funny little dance as part of his run-up. It's the sort of thing that comes naturally to players like Ronaldinho and Thierry Henry but for someone as artless as Jeff Whitley, it just made him look like an idiot. Naturally, the penalty was saved, Michael Hughes converted the next one for Palace and it was all over.

McCarthy shuffled his pack in the summer of 2004 and bought brilliantly, understanding perfectly what was needed to prosper in what had now been renamed as the Football League Championship. Still needing to be thrifty, he brought in Newcastle's centre half Stephen Caldwell, midfielders Liam Lawrence, Dean Whitehead and Carl Robinson and highly-rated young Irish striker Stephen Elliott, the latter of whom had been on the brink of breaking into the Manchester City first team. They replaced out of contract players such as McAteer, Bjorklund and Tommy Smith, and McCarthy got the quintet for a sum total of £450,000.

They helped the side secure the Championship at a canter, winning 29 out of their 46 league games.

The side started slowly again, winning only one of their first six games, but once they hit their stride they never looked back.

Dumbarton's Neill Collins was added to the squad for £25,000 and Danny Collins came from Chester for £140,000. McCarthy was the perfect manager for Sunderland at that time – the club was up to its neck in around £40 million of debt and here was a manager who was fashioning a winning side out of the pennies he had to spend in the transfer market.

The manager instilled a ferocious team spirit and an addictive winning mentality, engineered a settled back four, and founded a midfield where the central players worked relentlessly while the wide men got forward whenever they could to provide Stewart and Elliott with the ammunition they needed to score goals.

An early-season 1-0 win at promotion rivals Leeds was the side's fourth straight victory and laid down a marker to the Yorkshire club and the rest of the league, letting them know that Sunderland now had a side that was to be reckoned with. The squad was enhanced by the return of Michael Bridges who had been released by Leeds, Newcastle and Bolton following a horrific run of long-term injuries. The Sunderland faithful were largely delighted at the return of the prodigal son, but McCarthy could find no room for him in the starting line-up and the forward was mostly restricted to cameo appearances from the bench.

It was a poor league, and McCarthy had found that essential blend of grit and flair in a well-shaped team who kicked on in the middle of January with a run of 11 wins in 13 games, lifting them right into the promotion race. Wigan were out in front but overtaking them was inevitable. The final match of that 13-game run was at Wigan, with promotion almost within reach – 7,500 Sunderland fans travelled to Lancashire, taking over the whole of the main stand at the JJB Stadium. Marcus Stewart put Sunderland ahead after just three minutes and they never looked back afterwards, chalking up their eighth straight win, a blinding run of form that came just at the right time.

Promotion was confirmed with a 2-1 win at the Stadium of Light over Leicester City with two games remaining, and the Championship was wrapped up the following week in front of the TV cameras at West Ham. Stephen Elliott sealed the result and the league title with a fantastic curling shot as the seconds ticked away.

Although they had made it back into the big time, the paying public hadn't been completely bowled over and crowds averaged just under 29,000 for the season.

An almost impossible job followed as Mick McCarthy tried to assemble a side that would be able to hang on in the Premiership. Chairman Bob Murray made it clear from the outset that there would be precious little money available for strengthening the side and talk of contracts with clauses leading to wage cuts in the event of relegation made it look as though McCarthy was almost trying to put together a team that would be able to challenge for promotion again in a year's time. The contract policy was born of necessity given the club's debt.

What money McCarthy did have, he spent badly. A lack of a decent foreign scouting network, added to some wrong-headed desire to 'buy British' meant that the club were operating with one hand tied behind their back and a built-in defeatist attitude. But the way the manager spent his £4 million transfer budget was at best alarming. Almost half of the cash was blown on Blackburn striker Jon Stead, who had scored just twice in 29 games the previous season and was still waiting for his first Sunderland goal as 2006 loomed into view. Stead is the classic example of a confidence player, and with that in mind, the Stadium of Light was the last place he needed to be.

Another million was splashed out on Ipswich 'keeper Kelvin Davis – what Davis lacked in ability in terms of kicking, dealing with crosses, rushing out and communicating with his defenders, he more than made up for with his... er, nope, sorry, there was nothing else. But Kelvin wasn't afraid to stand up and cop his share of the blame when appropriate – taking the rap for a late equaliser conceded against West Brom because he had lost his voice.

Then there was Andy Gray. Regarded by fans young and old as one of the worst players to ever turn out for the club (and there'd certainly been some competition down the years), Gray's role seemed to be as a quirky target man incapable of winning headers while committing stacks of fouls into the bargain. McCarthy squandered almost a million pounds on Gray from a delighted Sheffield

United, and before the season was over he was heading back to the Championship with a loan spell at Burnley. Alan Stubbs arrived from Everton, realised he'd made a horrible, horrible mistake and quickly scarpered back to Goodison.

As 2005–06 got underway, it was quickly apparent that Sunderland were in fact a pale shadow of the previous year's Championship winning team, second best all over the park in every game they played. It was hard to believe that Sunderland had been significantly superior to Wigan and West Ham the season before, both of whom had coped admirably with the challenges of the Premiership.

After losing at home against Chelsea on January 15th, Sunderland had amassed a grand total of six points from 21 league games. Looking back, the 19 point season from a couple of years before seemed like a rollercoaster ride of thrills and spills. Add together McCarthy's zero-point tally from the end of that season, and the manager had acquired six points out of a possible 90 during his time as a Premiership manager with Sunderland.

Because he was blunt and avuncular, McCarthy got away with it for far longer than he should have. In the eyes of the supporters, Bob Murray was the real bad guy for allowing the club's finances to fall into such disrepute. Murray was to blame for a lot of things, but fans would have been equally upset if he'd meddled in the transfer dealings of Peter Reid that started the snowball of tragedy that grew throughout the early part of the 21st century.

Where Murray went wrong was to put his blind faith in Reid without realising that the game was up. Giving Reid almost £20 million to spend in the summer of 2002 and then sacking him nine games into the season was idiotic, but Murray had done it before on a smaller scale with Denis Smith just over a decade before.

Back in 2006, and McCarthy seemed to be completely bereft of ideas. Offers of help from sports psychologists were chucked in the bin – although probably because the club couldn't afford to pay them for their services (by that point they could scarcely afford the bin.) The manager's method of breeding stars from the lower leagues that had served Sunderland so well in the Championship was exposed as naïve and unfeasible in the Premiership and as rumours of an imminent takeover bid from Niall Quinn grew, McCarthy was sacked in March 2006 with Sunderland and their ten points the laughing stock of football.

Old warhorse Kevin Ball was fast-tracked from the youth academy to look after the first team until the end of the season and he added a further five points to the tally, including a win over Fulham in Sunderland's final home match of the season. Almost unthinkably, it was their only home win of the campaign. The football club was on its knees – bring on The Irish Uprising.

CHAPTER FOURTEEN

TAXIS TO THE TOP

IN THE WEEK following the crucial win at West Brom, Roy Keane took his players for a day of white water rafting in Stockton-on-Tees. Earlier in the season it might have been a convenient way to 'lose' one or two stragglers from the squad, but by now everyone was pulling in the same direction and it acted as a good exercise in team bonding.

Niall Quinn was trying a different kind of bonding – the chairman was touring pubs and clubs of the north east, in a bid to persuade lapsed supporters to come back to the Stadium of Light and give the players the extra lift that would be needed as they edged closer to promotion.

Addressing a total of 7,000 fans he urged those who had turned their backs to return and help make the club great again. The chairman spoke of his faith in Roy Keane, Drumaville's plans for wiping out the club's debts over the coming decade, and a summer transfer kitty in excess of £10 million – more if promotion was achieved. He also announced that fans who bought their season tickets early could pay the current season's prices, interest free over a ten month period. A bargain, if Sunderland were going to be back in the Premier League by August.

The first team squad were also on the road, or at least most of them were. As the squad prepared to travel down to Barnsley ahead of the match at Oakwell, Anthony Stokes, Tobias Hysen and Marton Fulop were left behind by Keane after failing to arrive at the Academy of Light at the designated time. When he took on the job back in August, Roy Keane had said that all he wanted from his players was for them to turn up on time and do their best. Punctuality is obviously something he holds dear, and the ruthless way in which he left behind three important players will have sent a message to the rest of the squad – if they weren't already tuned into the Keane way of doing things that is.

It could have been a catastrophic decision if a weakened Sunderland had failed to do the business, particularly as Carlos Edwards and Dwight Yorke were already missing through injury. Those players that did make it onto the pitch at Oakwell got the job done, even if it took a while to crack a determined and disciplined Barnsley defence.

Grant Leadbitter got a place in the starting line-up, on the right of midfield, possibly at the expense of Stokes, and the young midfielder took his chance, breaking the deadlock on 66 minutes. Murphy made a surging run towards the Barnsley box before laying the ball off to Leadbitter, who's not afraid of hitting a shot from distance. His luck was in and the ball was in the back of the net, to the relief of the 8,000-strong red and white army who had all arrived on time for the early kick-off.

Barnsley were struggling near the foot of the table and could not afford to lose the match. Their best efforts came from launching aimless balls forward which the Black Cats' defence dealt with easily, and one of those led to Sunderland's second. A long headed clearance forward from Jonny Evans reached David Connolly, and with the Barnsley defence stretched, he checked back on himself on the edge of their area and slotted a shot between two defenders past the 'keeper's right hand and into the back of the net. An ugly victory but a pleasing one.

After the match, Keane praised the players' spirit while criticising those who had missed the bus on the way to Barnsley. 'I've been at the club six months and there's been a number of players who were late,' he said. 'If there's a genuine reason, no problem. But when it happens more than once, there's something seriously wrong.'

Keane himself, of course, once kept Jack Charlton and the Irish team waiting on one well-publicised morning in 1991. They were due off at 7.30am, Keane turned up at 8am. Asked about it after this match, Keane stared at his questioner for several long seconds before speaking. 'Are you saying there's one rule for me and and a different one for the players? Don't patronise me. Get your facts straight, I was never late for a match'.

At the start of the following week he was at pains to point out that there would be no grudges and the matter was forgotten. Keane revealed that, 'The rest of the squad were ripping the three lads all day on Sunday because they've never been so early for training. Of course they were on time, more than on time. They were that early they brought the milk in.'

The Sunday training session acted as preparation for a midweek home match against Stoke City. Earlier in the season, at the Britannia Stadium, the Potters' strong physical side had out-muscled Sunderland and taken all three points in a 2-1 win. They tried a similar approach on Wearside and almost got away with the same result.

Stoke hadn't created a single notable chance by the time they took the lead, when Darel Russell's first time drive from over 25 yards out was spilled by Darren Ward, bobbling out of the 'keeper's clutches and trickling over his goal line. It was a rare mistake for Ward who had been expected to warm the bench when he arrived but who had become a huge part of Sunderland's rise up the table. Shocked, the Black Cats gathered themselves and were level again a minute later. Leadbitter's inswinging cross from the right was cleverly chested down by David Connolly into the path of the oncoming Dean Whitehead who lashed a first time shot past on target to even up the score.

Stoke weren't daunted by losing their lead so quickly and came back for more in an even-handed first half. The visitors upset everyone's evening by taking the lead again right on half-time. Carl Hoefkens evaded the attentions of the Sunderland defenders just inside the Sunderland penalty area, edging the ball away from Collins before blasting the ball high into the net and putting Stoke 2-1 up.

In the second half, Sunderland came out looking for an equaliser, but the sheer physicality of the Stoke side (Liam Lawrence excepted) stopped them from taking control of the game in the manner to which they were becoming accustomed. Sunderland though had picked up the ability to keep grafting right to the end and, as at Barnsley, Burnley and Hull, a late goal spared their blushes.

Right on 90 minutes, a cross from the left by Leadbitter sailed over the mass of bodies in the middle of the Stoke area. Nyron Nosworthy jumped and nudged it on to where Murphy had found some space on the right, the Irishman sweeping a fierce left-foot shot into the net and relieving the crowd of all their built-up tension.

The fans felt that a winner was there for the taking when four added minutes were announced and the Black Cats persevered, but a shot from Leadbitter flashed wide and that was as close as they got. There was no shame in a draw, and the unbeaten league run now stretched to twelve games. Derby and Birmingham had also dropped points that night and a great chance to move closer to the top two had disappeared.

Four days on, Sunderland had another chance to close on the top two before an enforced break for international fixtures. St Patrick's Day saw the arrival of Hull City to Wearside and whereas it took Sunderland 90 minutes to score against the Tigers on Humberside back in October, they were off the mark within three minutes.

Jonny Evans had missed the second half of the Stoke match with blurred vision following a bang on the head, but his sight was restored sufficiently for him to see Dean Whitehead's right-sided free-kick travel deep into the Hull penalty box. Evans rose the highest to give the ball that extra momentum needed to divert it sailing over the 'keeper's head and Sunderland were off to the perfect start.

Hull were in trouble at the bottom end of the table and most would have expected them to crumble after going behind so early. It wasn't the case and although they never threatened Darren Ward's goal, a combination of good defending and sloppy Sunderland finishing meant it was the final minute before unsettled fans could breathe easily and turn their thoughts to Guinness.

Hull 'keeper Boaz Myhill sliced a clearance right at the death which Stern John collected before steadying himself, taking his time to control the ball and advance on the 'keeper who had recovered his position. John promptly took the ball around Myhill and rolled it into an empty net.

It was 33 points out of a possible 39 for Sunderland and they moved up the table a notch, finally making it to second spot. It wasn't to last long, as Birmingham weren't playing until the following day, but the Blues' 1-1 draw with West Bromwich Albion meant that Sunderland were creeping closer to their target. Maintain their form and promotion would surely be their's.

Keane praised his players' performance but when asked about a possible permanent deal for the outstanding Jonny Evans, the manager quipped that he'd spoken to Sir Alex Ferguson about the possibility of signing the defender but that there was 'probably more chance of England's cricketers winning the World Cup.'

After the international break, Sunderland got back down to business with a trip to Cardiff City, more than four months since their last league defeat. Ninian Park is a nasty, old-fashioned ground, and a selection of the Cardiff support has an attitude to match. All well and good – the atmosphere wins them more points than it loses them every season and there's no rule which says clubs have to roll out the red carpet for opposing teams.

On a day when the weather matched the surroundings, a gusting wind and rain showers restricted either side from playing any fancy stuff. It's the hallmark of a successful team when they can win with nice, flowing football but also roll their sleeves up and dig in for an ugly win when required, and Sunderland did just that in Wales. They were the better side in the opening exchanges but Cardiff showed their resolve before half-time testing Darren Ward on a couple of occasions.

The game turned in the 57th minute when Ross

Wallace replaced Tobias Hysen. The Swede wasn't having one of his best days and fortunately Wallace was about to. The Scottish winger scored the game's only goal in the 72nd minute, from a free-kick curled in from the right, straight through Cardiff's comical attempt at a defensive wall.

Sunderland earned three more points but gained no further ground on Derby or Birmingham as both sides also won. For Sunderland fans, the day was one of the most memorable of the season, but not for the football. Nyron Nosworthy had been a cult figure among the fans virtually since the day he arrived, although not just for football. Nosworthy had been transformed in recent months since Keane switched him from full back to centre half, and the partnership he had built up with Jonny Evans had been a major component in Sunderland's rise up the table since the turn of the year.

The fans, Keane and Nosworthy himself had all been aware of the defender's limitations and Keane joked that 'now that Nos has switched to centre-back, he's got much less time on the ball. Which is best for all concerned.'

At Cardiff, during another party atmosphere among the travelling Sunderland support, Nyron earned himself a song – to the tune of the Amy Winehouse hit *Rehab*, the red and white army inserted the words:

> *'They tried to take the ball past Nyron;*
> *he said no, no, no.'*

The party atmosphere would travel on to Bristol airport later in the evening leading to an incredible set of circumstances that would have enshrined Niall Quinn as a Sunderland legend for life – had he not been one already. The fans, were in a celebratory mood as they sat on board waiting for their 9.25pm Bristol to

Newcastle flight to take off. They saw Quinn and burst into spontaneous song.

> *'Niall Quinn's disco pants are the best.*
> *They go up from his arse to his chest.*
> *They're better than Adam and the Ants.*
> *Niall Quinn's disco pants!'*

This boisterous behaviour was suddenly deemed to be a security risk and a dozen passengers were removed from the aircraft, supposedly for drunkenness, although one suffered from learning difficulties and another had a false leg, which he triumphantly waved above his head as he left the plane.

The Sunderland chairman was also off the plane minutes later, although of his own volition. Easyjet then announced that the flight had been cancelled leaving 80 fans stranded in Bristol airport with no further flights due until the morning. Quinn had told airline staff, 'These are my people. You cannot treat them like that,' and he wasn't going to stand by and let them be messed around on the whim of a few over-officious cabin stewards.

The chairman summoned a fleet of taxis to take the fans the full 300 miles back home at a personal cost of over £8,000 – a unique and noble gesture in a football world where fans are nowadays treated as consumers to be fleeced at every opportunity. It was further evidence of Quinn's yearning to reconnect the club and its fans.

Coming five days before the deadline for fans to snap up 2007–08 season tickets at bargain Championship prices, the timing of the Easyjet fiasco was a spin doctor's dream. The only way that Niall Quinn could have generated more positive publicity would be if he'd hijacked the plane, bound and gagged the Easyjet crew before single-handedly flying the thing back to the north east armed only with a copy of 'The Dummies' Guide To Amateur Aviation'. Oh, and arranged for everyone to be parachuted into their back gardens of course.

In the not-too-distant future, look out for less scrupulous chairmen rescuing toddlers from lakes, pulling blind pensioners from burning buildings and other spectacularly heroic feats just when it's time for their disillusioned fans to dig deep and shell out for another year of chronic underachievement.

In the days following the launch of Quinn's Taxis, business at the Stadium of Light ticket office was frenetic. The penny finally dropped for hordes of stay-away supporters and fans were being forced to stand and queue for as long as two hours to sign up for the following season.

As April arrived, Roy Keane collected another manager of the month award, with slightly more grace and an apology for his comment that he would be putting February's award in his garage. The Easter bank holiday weekend beckoned, with two games in short succession, and potentially a make or break period for the three teams who had now eased away from the pack and were jostling for the pair of automatic promotion places and the financial rewards that come with them.

The momentum leading up to the Wolves match got an added boost on Good Friday when Derby took a short trip across the Midlands to Leicester and were found wanting. The Foxes were still not entirely certain of safety and offered up a fairly toothless display for most of the game, falling behind in the first half before rallying in the second and sneaking an unexpected equaliser. At the final whistle, both teams took a point each, a frustrating day's business for Derby and further evidence that the pressure Sunderland had been putting on them in recent weeks was beginning to affect them.

The Black Cats would go into the following day's Wolves match knowing that a win would take them to within a point of Derby and that golden ticket to the Premiership. But Mick McCarthy was coming back and he'd have a very different plan for the afternoon.

Wolves pitched up on Wearside on the back of a diabolical 6-0 whacking at home at the hands of Southampton the previous weekend. That, added to McCarthy's return and the fact that Sunderland's unbeaten league run was entering its fourth month (and as everyone knows, unbeaten runs are there to be broken), led to an air of slight unease at odds with the red and white bandwagon that was gripping the city.

A big result was desperately required. It was essential that the ghost of the McCarthy regime was buried, and anyway, there was a busload of Trinidad fans heading north from London, all drawn to the club following the signings of Yorke, Edwards and John. A steel band was scheduled to play by the statue of Bob Stokoe ahead of kick-off – a magnificent thought, but something that never came off after the Trini fans' coach from London was delayed, apparently due to an excessive amount of toilet stops on the way up!

Fittingly for the Caribbean visitors, the sun blazed down on Wearside and the crowd was an impressive 40,748, the biggest Championship attendance of the season. Not unexpectedly, Keane shuffled his pack yet again, and the most pleasing change was the premature return of Carlos Edwards on the right side of midfield, back a good three or four games earlier than had been expected. Ross Wallace got a well-earned start following his winner at Cardiff, taking the place of Tobias Hysen, who along with Dwight Yorke and Anthony Stokes, failed even to make the 16. The boss obviously had Monday's long trip to Southampton in mind, as David Connolly was dropped to the bench, alongside Stephen Elliott, who was making his latest comeback from long-term injury.

Sunderland started quickly, looking to impose themselves on the game from the first kick, but refreshingly, Wolves had come to play football as opposed to getting men behind the ball and trying to frustrate a result out of the home side. But Keane's team were in the ascendancy and went ahead after quarter of an hour.

Wide on the left, Ross Wallace sent a ball into the left-hand side of the box to Daryl Murphy. A combination of luck and skill saw it spin up off Murphy – he reacted quicker than Neill Collins and brought it down before lashing it into the net from a tight angle.

Sunderland had chances to add further goals in the first half but Wolves 'keeper Matt Murray kept them at bay. The Midlanders started the second half with more purpose and an equaliser looked on the cards until Sunderland crafted a fantastic second goal. Murphy, out on the right flank, bent in a lovely left-footed cross. Ross Wallace had ghosted in from the left-hand side and headed it back across the 'keeper, putting clear daylight between the two sides.

After doing all the hard work and creating a two-goal cushion, some dozy defending by Sunderland allowed Andy Keogh to get a powerful header onto a Michael McIndoe cross and bring it back to 2-1 again. From then on, both sides had realistic chances to score and it was a nerve-wracking ending to the match for the Stadium of Light regulars as well as those who had been inspired to come back to support the side.

As the final whistle went and the crowd dispersed,

the PA system played the theme from *Taxi* as a tribute to the chairman. To cap it all, a late result from St Andrews revealed that Birmingham had been beaten at home by Burnley, elevating Sunderland into second place and edging the team nearer to automatic promotion.

The second part of the intense double-dose of football that is traditionally served up over the Easter holiday weekend came on Bank Holiday Monday, with a delayed kick-off time of 5.15pm, as the long trip to Southampton was being broadcast by Sky. This put Sunderland at a distinct advantage as both Derby and Birmingham played earlier in the afternoon, and the suspicion that the wheels were starting to come off for both sides was further confirmed as Birmingham lost 1-0 at Barnsley, with most of the players becoming embroiled in a mass brawl after the final whistle.

Almost as heartening was the news that Derby had floundered yet again, a point in a 1-1 draw against Coventry the best they could muster. With Sunderland still to play their second match of the weekend, they had already garnered more points in total than their two rivals, and by engineering a win at St Mary's they would find themselves top of the table for the first time since winning the Championship two years ago, and with their destiny entirely in their hands from then on in.

Not surprisingly, Roy Keane made changes from the Wolves match just 48 hours previously – what was surprising though was that the two players who had scored against Wolves stepped down from the starting line-up. Daryl Murphy was on the bench while Ross Wallace dropped out of the 16 altogether. In came Connolly and Stephen Elliott up front, and Dwight Yorke returned to central midfield taking the place (and captain's armband) from Dean Whitehead.

If Sunderland fans expected the team to be fortified

from the afternoon's other results and to take to the field before clinically picking up the three points and sailing to the top of the league, then they were to be mistaken. Slightly.

The match started at a furious pace, with neither side afforded the opportunity to dwell on the ball or create many real openings. Both teams worked hard to close down play whenever they could and by the break, Sunderland had failed to even register a shot on target, Yorke being the worst culprit, putting a free header over the bar in a move that seemed to go in slow motion. However, viewers at home were tickled by the inane ramblings of Sky's 'expert' analyst, Chris Kamara, who seemed to think that Carlos Edwards was predominantly a right-back and was doing well in his unfamiliar role on the wing.

As the second half got underway, the furious pace failed to abate. Keane made a couple of changes, withdrawing Elliott as the player eased his way back towards match fitness. Dean Whitehead also came on in a straight swap for Liam Miller. As the minutes ticked by, Southampton began to apply more and more pressure in the Black Cats' half and it wasn't the biggest surprise when the Saints took the lead in the 67th minute, Polish striker Marek Saganowski turning the ball in from eight yards after it was played to him by Danny Guthrie.

Perhaps the time had come for Sunderland's impressive unbeaten run to come to an end. Maybe, like Birmingham and Derby, they were about to fall foul of what Sir Alex Ferguson once memorably referred to as 'squeaky-bum time'.

As the game restarted, Southampton pressed on for a second, match-clinching goal but this also left them vulnerable to counter-attacks. If there's one thing

Keane's Sunderland side revelled in, it was the chance to play football against a side who would also play an open game, and this was what was on offer now. It was also a game that had been played at a fast tempo, and was the second in a crammed weekend for both teams. The sort of game that would be decided by stamina and the quality of substitutions made by either side.

Carlos Edwards had acquitted himself well, not just in his attacking play but in his work-rate and ability to help snuff out the threat posed by Gareth Bale, Southampton's 17-year-old attacking left-back, the boy with a £10 million price tag on his head. Bale was nowhere to be seen when Edwards picked the ball up on the right-hand side about 40 yards out from goal, and the Southampton defence clearly hadn't done their homework when they allowed the Sunderland winger to advance with it. Without even looking up, he put his left foot through the ball and half a second later it was in the top right-hand corner of the Saints' net.

Parity restored, Sunderland smelled blood. This would truly be the point when stamina and subs sorted the men from the boys. With 85 minutes on the clock, Grant Leadbitter, who had replaced the sweat-drenched Yorke, also found himself outside the area with a crucial amount of time and space.

Leadbitter took a touch to get the ball from under his feet before sweetly lashing it past Saints 'keeper Bartosz Bialkowski's left hand and into the back of the net. Again, Southampton had been slow to react to a situation which they didn't judge as dangerous, and again they had been punished. The goals had come from the two midfielders who are more than capable of scoring from distance and on both occasions they did just that.

Once Leadbitter had bagged Sunderland's second

there was little time for Southampton to rally themselves and come looking for a way back into the match. After a drawn-out five minutes of stoppage time, the referee blew for time and Sunderland were top of the Championship, with just four games left to play. The timing could scarcely have been better. After just over seven months in charge and 37 league games, Roy Keane had hauled Sunderland from the doldrums of the bottom of the table right up to the very top. Promotion was within touching distance. Sunderland's destiny was in their own hands.

CHAPTER FIFTEEN

WEAR ON OUR WAY

THE WINS OVER Wolves and Southampton in the space of just over 48 hours had set up the climax of Sunderland's season perfectly, giving the team complete control of their own destiny. Victory in each of their next four matches and they would be promoted. Winning three out of the four would almost certainly seal it – taking Birmingham and Derby's late season form into account; two wins from four would probably do the trick.

As Sunderland hit the top of the Championship, moves were being made off the field to take the club to a new level. A major new sponsorship deal was struck with Ireland's largest independent bookmaker, Boyle Sports. As well as the four-year deal, the company would also provide betting facilities through the club's official website and within the Stadium of Light. A new kit deal had also been negotiated, with Umbro, and more and more companies were eager to be affiliated with the club as their profile within the football world continued to grow.

Niall Quinn's heroic gesture in shelling out £8,000 in taxi fares to get stranded fans home from Bristol Airport had captured the imagination and given both Quinn and the club some positive press coverage. Fans had also needed help getting home after the following away game at Southampton. Saints fans had hurled missiles at the windows of one of the supporters' coaches – when club officials heard about this, they turned around the players' coach and sent it back to pick up the fans on the damaged bus.

Sunderland's next opponents, QPR, had themselves hit a run of form, winning three out of their previous four matches, and easing themselves away from a relegation scare. Another big crowd, just short of 40,000, made their way to the Stadium of Light, willing the team on towards the finishing line.

Ahead of the game, the manager heaped high praise on his squad, saying, 'The players are getting their just rewards. You've got to work hard to win football matches. I've been involved in good teams since I was eight years old and in terms of work-rate, this team is second to none.' Keane had previously told the players that if they scored twice in each match, they would be promoted, and they seemed to be following his instructions to the letter – they had finished seven out of their last eight games with two goals. Against QPR they would do it again.

After making only the bench at Southampton, Dean Whitehead was restored to the starting line-up, and it took the skipper just seven minutes to put Sunderland in front. Nyron Nosworthy played the ball upfield to David Connolly, who laid it into the path of Whitehead who had broken from midfield, racing through to fire the ball past Lee Camp in the QPR goal.

One-nil, and the third consecutive home match in which Sunderland had taken the lead in the opening 15 minutes. The early goal fired them up and they were soon in complete control, with QPR's role restricted to trying to stem the tide of the Wearsiders' attacking play.

But Whitehead had a major hand in the Londoners' surprise equaliser after 23 minutes. His sloppy pass in midfield was pounced upon and within a couple of seconds QPR's leading goalscorer Dexter Blackstock was racing into Sunderland's 18-yard area. Darren Ward came out to meet him but clipped the forward and the referee pointed straight at the spot. Martin Rowlands stepped up and put it away. The scores were level, and Sunderland's march towards promotion was faltering.

They remained resolute, and continued to attack. Yorke, Connolly and Murphy all failed to convert glorious chances and the sides went in level at half-time when Sunderland should have been leading by four or five goals to one. QPR had offered nothing in the way of goalmouth threat other than the penalty while David Connolly had numerous opportunities to end his recent drought, now stretching to six games, but failed to make any of them count.

There was a wonderful moment midway through the second half which brilliantly illustrated the overpowering influence that Roy Keane has on players, and not necessarily those of Sunderland. As a young QPR player was about to take a free-kick on the left-hand side, Keane raced to his technical area and yelled something at the player. Startled, the youngster turned round, saw who was shouting at him and duly moved the free-kick back a few yards as he'd been ordered to do by Keane.

As Roy Keane's overhaul of Sunderland had lifted the team up the league, it had also raised the expectations of the supporters. Back in August, a point from a match like this would have been a decent result; avoiding embarrassment was the side's main priority; now, nothing less than a win would suffice.

At Southampton, Grant Leadbitter had come off the

bench and scored a dramatic winner with a long range shot. Against QPR five days later, he did the same. A quarter of an hour after being introduced to the game, Leadbitter lurked in space 25 yards from goal, right in the centre of the field. Carlos Edwards had the ball, preparing to take a free-kick on the right. Everyone expected a cross into the box, but Edwards merely rolled it sideways to Leadbitter – the youngster pulled off what was almost a carbon copy of his goal at St Mary's. The ball torpedoed straight into the bottom left-hand corner, rocking the Stadium of Light and keeping the promotion chase alive.

There was no looking back for the remainder of the game, and QPR had nothing to offer in return. It should never really have been as tight as it was – Sunderland should have won the match at a canter by half-time, but Sunderland fans have become used to the strain over the years. It beats supporting a team like, say, Fulham, who never do anything of note. In the decade at the Stadium of Light, there hasn't been a single season when there was nothing to play for towards the end. Promotion, relegation and even European qualification – one of those three has always been on the menu during or around every April.

Elsewhere, Birmingham and Derby had mixed fortunes, with the Blues winning 2-1 while the Rams lost by the same scoreline. Birmingham then won their midweek game in hand at Leicester, also by 2-1. This lifted them back into second place, just two points behind Sunderland with Derby four points behind the Wearsiders. It meant that if Derby lost against Luton that Friday evening, a Sunderland win at Colchester would clinch promotion. The worst case scenario was that the inevitable would be delayed until the following Friday, when Sunderland were to meet Burnley at the

Stadium of Light, live on Sky. That would be a fitting way to wrap things up.

As a break from usual training, Keane organised a squad trip to Swaledale. No one missed the bus although one or two might have wished they had, as they were faced with four hours of mountain biking up and down the hills of the region. There were a few sore individuals afterwards, including the manager, who said, 'I joined in, I made the effort and I'm paying for it today. The seats were like razor blades!'

As things turned out, Derby's 1-0 win over Luton meant that nothing would be settled at Colchester. In fact, Sunderland's promotion challenge might well have completely come off the rails when they lost 3-1. The match was always going to be a potential banana skin as Colchester's outstanding home record had taken them to the brink of the play-offs a year after promotion from League One. It was the end of the Black Cats' 17-game unbeaten run and it couldn't have come at a worse time.

Sunderland weren't at their best on the day, possibly still saddle-sore, but they were the better side, Colchester playing more like an away team, content to mop up Sunderland's pressure and launch breakaway attacks whenever they could. The visitors should have gone ahead just before the break when Connolly went close, but it was the U's who went in front, four minutes into what was supposed to be just three minutes of stoppage time. Wayne Brown, unmarked, headed in from a corner.

Sunderland raised their game at the start of the second half and were rewarded with an equaliser, Dwight Yorke heading home from Daryl Murphy's left-sided cross. At this stage, a point would have been a decent result but a win would have been ideal. In the end, Keane's men finished the afternoon with nothing. With just eight minutes left, Sunderland collapsed, Ehpraim and Guy combining well on the left before finding Garcia in the box. His turn eluded Evans before he put the ball in the back of the net.

Right at the death, the Wearsiders' fate was sealed when Colchester won a penalty after Whitehead fouled Jamie Cureton. The striker got up and took the penalty himself, sending Ward the wrong way and Sunderland home empty-handed and sweating on the prospect of still being in the top two by the end of the season. It was still all in Sunderland's hands though, as, although Birmingham went top again after beating Mick McCarthy's Wolves (thanks Mick!), Derby were still a point adrift in third place.

With two games to play, Birmingham were on 83 points, Sunderland on 82 and Derby County on 81. Any two from three could be promoted or become champions. It was now all down to who could hold their nerve. As Roy Keane said after the Colchester match, 'It is still in our hands. If we win the next two games, we will be OK.'

The next match at home to Burnley the following Friday couldn't now be a promotion party, but in front of a huge crowd, and with the TV cameras present, it would be one of the most memorable nights in a decade of football at the Stadium of Light, fired up by a 44,448 crowd (who were the four extra people who ruined the symmetry?)

With that special atmosphere that evening kick-offs add to a match, Sunderland were at their best from the beginning. Strutting confidently, they out-passed and outclassed a Burnley side who did well not to concede in the first ten minutes, as David Connolly had a couple of good chances to put Sunderland on their way that went begging.

No club who can draw around 45,000 fans for a televised match should be operating outside of the top flight and spurred on by the crowd, and an immense performance by Dean Whitehead in the centre of midfield, Sunderland took the lead in the 14th minute. Connolly beat his man on the left wing and sent in a low cross, finding Daryl Murphy in an ocean of space. The Irish striker put the ball in the net and, unsure if he was offside or not, checked with the referee's assistant. No flag – he'd timed his run to perfection, and Sunderland were a goal to the good.

Seven minutes later Connolly spurned a chance to double Sunderland's lead. The striker was fouled by Wayne Thomas in the Burnley penalty area, a tug of the shirt which the referee did well to see. A spot kick was awarded and it looked as though the game was going to be done and dusted in just over 20 minutes. Connolly stepped up but it wasn't the best penalty he'll ever take – Brian Jensen guessed right and had no trouble palming the ball away.

The shock of missing the penalty seemed to take the sting out of Sunderland's game and the pendulum started to swing away from them six minutes before half-time with another penalty, this time for Burnley. It was dubious at best. As Wade Elliott burst into the box, Darren Ward made the slightest of contact with him as he raced past.

The 'keeper was pulling out of the challenge at the last moment but Elliott needed no persuasion to go down and the match had its second penalty. Andy Gray, hopelessly out of his depth in the Premiership with Sunderland the season before but a reliable goal scorer at this level, sent Ward the wrong way and levelled the scores. Gray made the most of it, winding up the North Stand faithful with his celebration in front of them. Ah well, he was a Burnley player now and they don't get worshipped by 45,000 at Turf Moor.

It got worse five minutes after half-time. The game had hardly had time to settle down again when Wade Elliott picked the ball up a good 25 yards out and just leathered it, his shot bending away and out of the reach of Ward. The crowd fell into stunned silence. This definitely wasn't in the script.

Sunderland had dragged themselves up the table in the preceding eight months sometimes through sheer dogged determination, unity and an overpowering will to win. They now had about 40 minutes to do it again. Defeat would not be acceptable. A draw would look like weakness and act as encouragement for Birmingham and Derby to comfortably finish the job themselves.

The home side got down to the job in hand, urged on continuously by their supporters – if the adage is true about a crowd being a 12th man, they were certainly doing their bit here. Four minutes after going behind, the game's third penalty was awarded. Carlos Edwards beat his defender and brought the ball across the front of the box, closing in on Jensen.

As he went past him, the 'keeper got the feeblest of touches and Edwards went down. If the Burnley penalty was dubious, then so was this. But one dodgy penalty had evened out the other.

Connolly had no worries about stepping up again – he hit the ball to Jensen's right once more, but with far more purpose than his original effort. It was irrelevant. The 'keeper headed in the opposite direction as the ball bulged the net and the crowd erupted in celebration and relief. Up in the directors' box, Niall Quinn was out of his seat, throwing his arms into the air. On the touchline, Keane, wearing his best grey-tinged beard for the evening, was utterly unmoved. Later, Connolly, reflected on his efforts, saying, 'I think Dean Whitehead fancied the second penalty, and rightly so. [They] are pressure, but I wouldn't have been able to sleep at night if I'd shied away from taking the second one.'

Sunderland poured forward but left gaps in midfield, and Burnley had chances to take the lead for the second time. Keane added some fresh legs into the game, bringing on Leadbitter and Hysen for Miller and Stokes. Leadbitter would again be involved in wrapping up the points after coming off the bench, starting the move that led to Sunderland's best and most important goal of the season, and one that ranks up there with the finest strikes the Stadium of Light has ever seen.

With ten minutes to go and Sunderland still searching for the vital third goal, Grant Leadbitter picked up the ball deep inside Burnley's half, playing it quickly forward to Daryl Murphy, who found himself with acres of space to gallop into. As Burnley's defenders hared back and regained their positions, Murphy played the ball sideways to his right to an onrushing and unmarked Carlos Edwards. The winger took a touch to control the ball and tee it up before unleashing a screaming shot from 25 yards out which flew past Jensen and into the top right hand corner.

If you're a Sunderland fan, you'll never ever get tired of watching this goal. You could throw a party around it. The recipe is simple – drinks, a buffet, and a room full of the people you care about most. Then just get them all to gather round the TV for five or six hours while you all watch the goal over and over again. Play, rewind, play, rewind, seven or eight thousand times – it's impossible to get sick of watching it. DVDs of it should be handed out to sufferers of depression. Its ability to heal the world of warfare needs to be investigated as soon as possible. It was a good goal. Carlos Edwards got himself a booking for over-celebrating – he should have got a knighthood. Had there not been a net to stop it, the ball would have hit me full in the face... but I wouldn't have minded. I'd have been part of history.

The momentum was back with Sunderland again, and they were back on top of the league. It didn't last long as Birmingham beat Sheffield Wednesday the following day to regain top spot. The two results did make things more difficult for Derby County however, and the Rams would have to win at Crystal Palace that Sunday if they were to have a chance of still being in the chase for promotion on the season's final day.

That match was live on Sky, and Palace, who had taken four points from their two games with Sunderland, finally did the Wearsiders a favour, beating a listless Derby by two goals to nil. The previous 48 hours' results had clearly knocked whatever fight was remaining in the Derby side, and there were even some Sunderland fans at Selhurst Park, willing the home side to the victory that would seal promotion for the Black Cats.

To clinch promotion without kicking a ball is an odd sensation, but the job had been done, and there had been a glorious inevitability about it from around February onwards. There was still some unfinished business. If results on the last day of the season went the right way, Sunderland could go up as champions. Keane's men had to beat already-relegated Luton Town at Kenilworth Road and hope that their bogey team, Preston North End, could get at least a point against Birmingham at Deepdale.

Keane had let the players celebrate after promotion was sealed, saying, 'The players have been letting a bit of steam off. I've no problem with that. You have to switch off a bit and they've had time to do that.'

They were next to bottom when he arrived, and

Keane wouldn't be satisfied until the Championship trophy was at the Stadium of Light, so there was to be no slackening off. He warned, 'In the next few days, if they're not switched back on then they won't play on Sunday.'

Sunderland fans converged on Luton in their thousands with the locals taking the chance to line their pockets – some tickets for the home end were being sold for as much as £300 a go. It makes sense to miss out on the last game of the season when your team have already been relegated and earn yourself enough cash to help pay for a whole season ticket for the following campaign.

There may have been a few sore heads at the club as Keane made some interesting changes for the Luton match. Marton Fulop got a game and Stephen Wright played, marking his return from another long-term injury. Top scorer David Connolly was dropped to the bench.

Sunderland could give themselves a chance of winning the league only if they took all three points at Kenilworth Road and they ripped into Luton like a team possessed from the first whistle. With less than four minutes played and with many of the red and white-clad 'Luton' fans still struggling to locate their seats, Anthony Stokes picked up the ball in the wide left area and drifted infield.

He got as far as 25 yards from the goal with no effective challenge offered by the Luton defence before angling a pass into Daryl Murphy who had stationed himself on the edge of the box. Murphy's first touch was lousy but the Irishman fortunately bought a ricochet off a Luton defender straight into the path of the incoming form of Stokes who had gambled and continued with his run. The minds of the Hatters defenders seemed to be elsewhere and Stokes had no problem slotting the ball past Dean Brill, low to his left-hand side as the Luton defenders looked around at each other in a half-hearted search for someone to blame.

After six minutes it was 2-0. Dean Whitehead raked a 50-yard ball out to Carlos Edwards on the right which the winger bravely laid off into the path of Daryl Murphy, Edwards ending up on his backside in the process. Murphy turned onto his preferred left foot and with the Luton defenders still daydreaming, the Irishman drilled a vicious drive first time from 25 yards straight past the luckless Brill. Brill indeed.

Any doubts that Sunderland wouldn't take all three points and give themselves a chance of the title were allayed when they opened up a three-goal cushion two minutes into the second half, with Murphy getting his second of the afternoon. The Irishman had endured a disappointing spell as a Luton player earlier in his career, but he was enjoying being at Kenilworth Road that day. Stokes broke away down the left and slid the ball across to an unmarked Murphy in the middle of the six-yard box – his tap-in was probably the simplest of the ten goals he'd scored all season.

With no break in the deadlock at Preston, Sunderland were sitting on top of the table as it stood, but a Birmingham goal at any time could rob the Black Cats of the prize they'd worked so hard for after giving the rest of the league a head start back in August. Sunderland put the match beyond any doubt in the 77th minute with another contender for 'goal of the game.' Ross Wallace replaced Carlos Edwards and within three minutes he had rattled a 25-yard shot into the Luton net which Brill had no chance whatsoever of stopping.

Still, if Birmingham were to score, it would all be rendered meaningless. In the 85th minute at Deepdale, there was indeed, a goal. Simon Whaley raced onto a long ball and held off two defenders before putting the ball past the Birmingham 'keeper. One-nil to Preston. Birmingham would now need two in the last five minutes. It didn't happen.

Back at Luton, news swiftly spread around the ground that Birmingham were losing, and it was time to celebrate. Fittingly David Connolly's contribution to the party was his 13th goal of the season. He flicked on a Grant Leadbitter free-kick from the left hand touchline and rounded things off very nicely. The title had been clinched with five minutes of the season to play. As the final whistle blew, the party really got started with those who had played and those who had missed out on the day coming together on the pitch as the fans joined in around the ground.

The only dark cloud over the day was the absence of a trophy to be lifted. In their wisdom, the Football League had decided that the trophy would not be at Kenilworth Road as Birmingham were leading the table going into the final game. Additionally, there were concerns over spectator safety, a wholly implausible argument – as usual the safety card was played to cover the backside of some idiotic decision made by someone with no feeling for the game. Roy Keane was furious, saying 'It is a PR disaster that we did not pick it up today. The supporters paid good money to travel here to watch us. I don't think safety would have been a problem.'

It had earlier been announced that Nyron Nosworthy had won the fans' vote as player of the season, with Jonny Evans picking up the young player award. Indeed, Nosworthy was a candidate, but only for his performances from the turn of the year when he switched his position to centre half. Before then, he was mediocre at best – when he could actually get in the team, that is. Dean Whitehead, Darren Ward or David Connolly would have been more suitable recipients for their consistent performances right throughout the season.

Ultimately, it was irrelevant. The only statistic that mattered was the league position. First. Top. Champions. Roy Keane's achievement, to take on the job, his first as a manager, when the club was in such a critical condition, and to mould a raggle-taggle bunch of lightweights into Championship winners in eight months was nothing short of startling. But the really hard work was yet to come.

CHAPTER SIXTEEN

IN IT TO WIN IT

NOT A LOT of people know this, but Birmingham City manager Steve Bruce is also a published novelist. Back in the days when he was the boss at Huddersfield Town, he wrote three books, engrossing works of fiction imaginatively entitled *Sweeper*, *Striker* and *Defender*, which follow the career of a familiar-sounding Steve Barnes, a former defender with Mulcaster United who has gone on to manage lowly Leddersford Town. In one of the books, he guides his team to dizzying success while trying to disprove accusations that he murdered one of his strikers. The recent history of Sunderland AFC could act as valuable source material for another Steve Barnes novel.

In a nutshell, the plot would go like this; a goal-scoring hero falls in love with the last club he plays for before retirement. Once he leaves, the club sink into a quagmire of perpetual failure until they are on the brink of ruin. The player puts together a consortium of businessmen and saves the club, promising to make it great again and take the supporters on a 'magic carpet ride'.

Unfortunately, the player (now chairman) can't find anyone who'll actually manage the club so he does it himself for a while, with disastrous consequences. Further on-the-field decline looks imminent.

There's more. The chairman identifies the man he wants to manage the team for him, a former playing colleague. Only problem is, the ex-player in question has no managerial experience whatsoever and is a notorious hot-head and former booze hound. He and the chairman haven't spoken to each other in four years since they fell out during the world's biggest tournament. Tentatively, their relationship is healed and the hot-head agrees to take over the management of the team.

Once the hot-head is installed in the hot-seat, he brings in half a dozen new players in the space of 48 hours, discarding most of those signed by the chairman in the preceding few weeks, as he doesn't feel they're good enough. One of the new players is a playboy millionaire with an estranged child stemming from a previous relationship with a top tabloid-hogging glamour model. The playboy couldn't be more unlike the dour manager but somehow it works. Under the new manager, the team start well but then struggle to find any kind of form and fans grow impatient. Some of the players are revealed to be amateur wannabe porn stars and are quickly transferred out of the club.

Still frustrated by the quality of his squad, the manager buys yet more players, some of whom are friends of the playboy millionaire. He then pulls a masterstroke by converting one of his underachieving defenders from a full back to a centre half. Previously, the player in question was something of a figure of fun, enthusiastic but severely limited and prone to on-field mistakes. But in his new position he is transformed overnight and becomes the heartbeat of the side, who by now, haven't lost a game in weeks.

Their amazing run of form continues. After winning a match located so far away that fans have to make a plane journey just to get to it, there is a fracas on their return flight as it is preparing to take off. The chairman is also on the plane and is appalled by the attitude of the airline staff. Unwilling to see the fans of his club stranded, he pulls out his credit card and pays for everyone to get home in a fleet of taxis, a journey of over 300 miles and at personal cost to himself of £8,000.

The team are still winning matches left, right and centre. One of the new players, a friend of the playboy millionaire turns out to have the hardest shot in the world – perhaps he has enchanted boots? The team slowly climb up the league and are in serious contention to win promotion at the end of the season. Just when it looks as though there will be a happy ending, they travel to the smallest, shabbiest ground in the league – a world away from their own palatial home, and are finally beaten! Their chances of winning promotion are now hanging in the balance. They return to their home ground and in front of a full house, win their next match 3-2. The winning goal is scored by the winger with the magic boots – the shot almost bursts the net but doesn't, saving the lives of scores of terrified but jubilant fans.

Promotion is finally confirmed two days later, but the team still have the chance to go on and win the league outright. To do so, they must win and hope that their deadliest rivals either draw or lose. The hot-headed manager has prepared his boys well and they win 5-0. Meanwhile, their rivals lose 1-0 with only five minutes of the season remaining, completing the rags to riches story of the club who were on their knees just eight months before. Oh, and the name of the manager of the club who threw away the league title right at the end? It's only the former Mulcaster United legend and ex-Leddersford Town boss Steve Barnes. It's a funny old game football, isn't it?

Shortly after he'd pulled off what, back in August, looked to be the impossible task of winning the league, Roy Keane not surprisingly announced that he wouldn't be resting on his laurels, saying, 'We've managed to get into the Premiership now and I'm not one for hanging around – let's get on with it and see how we go.' He firmly rejected plans for an open-topped bus parade through the city centre to celebrate the title win and was right to do so. Sunderland has had too many of them in recent years, and the reason they keep on having them is because the club keep on failing when they get to the next level. Secondary success is no success at all – it's just a façade.

Towards the end of the 2006/2007 season, Sunderland's Swedish midfielder Tobias Hysen revealed that Keane had set them their target for the remainder of the campaign almost as soon as he arrived – winning the league. To players who had lost their first five matches, including a cup-tie at Bury, (were then bottom of League Two,) that must have sounded like the craziest thing they'd ever heard. But if Keane hadn't believed it and hadn't said it, they would never have done it. Although he had a blank managerial CV, Keane knew where he was headed from the very beginning. Niall Quinn later said, 'We felt we'd have to nurse him along, put structures in place and give him every opportunity to develop and learn his trade. But lo and behold, he's astonished everyone and done it in record time.'

Roy Keane has shown that as a manager he is an absolute natural. As a player, he always professed to not being much cop, casting himself as a grafter, an artisan, whose fierce application and desire for self-improvement was the secret behind any success he might have had. He has shown the same qualities as a manager – the difference is that the period of preparation for management has been going on for two decades. He'd probably been quietly managing Manchester United inside his own head in all the time he was at the club – the players he railed against in the infamous MUTV interview that led to his hurried departure from Old Trafford in November 2005 would either have been moved on long before his outburst or not signed in the first place if he'd been the boss.

Right from day one at Sunderland he identified the changes that would need to be made immediately. The Academy of Light, one of the best in the country and built at huge cost was deemed to be more like a hospital. Immediately, the walls would be adorned with pictures of the club's former triumphs, so that the young trainees could get a sense of what their long-term goals would be as part of the club.

Under the new regime, the squad began staying together in a hotel the night before home matches as well as away ones, and would be seen travelling wearing club blazers instead of tracksuits. Nothing would be too good for Keane's players when it came to their all-round care and match preparation. Still smarting from having to suffer third-rate conditions when representing Ireland while being used to world-class facilities at Manchester United, Keane knew which method led to success and which led to failure.

Now, with the first part of the job done, comes the next challenge. The newly-renamed Premier League. Such is the gulf between the top flight and the Championship that the managers of most promoted clubs go into the season talking of reaching the magical tally of 40 points, the figure that should ensure survival for another season. Most don't get that far, either falling short and being relegated or copping for the sack on the way. Keane has no time for such small-minded defeatism. If the best you can aspire to is fourth from bottom then you might as well not bother in the first place.

Neither he or Niall Quinn have publicly set any targets for their first season as chairman and manager in the top flight, but they certainly won't have spent the summer chewing their finger nails and agonising over whether they'll be able to take the club as high as 17th in the league. Wisely, Quinn has said that there'll be no promises of success – he knows how easy that kind of talk can come back to haunt you.

When Bob Murray told Sunderland fans that the team would never be relegated from the Premiership again, they believed him and not without good reason. Forty-five thousand fans were pouring into the Stadium of Light every week and the club had the top goalscorer in Europe. Success would obviously breed success. Unfortunately it didn't and some gross mismanagement saw Sunderland end up beating their own record as the worst team in the history of the Premiership. To hold that record and then smash it three years later is pretty spectacular. Actually, it probably belongs in a Steve Barnes book.

Whatever anyone thinks of Bob Murray, it can't be denied that as Sunderland make the leap into the Premier League for the third time since moving into the Stadium of Light, the infrastructure of the club is second to none, and all Quinn and Keane have to worry about is getting it right on the field.

The staff at the much-mooted, but previously under-funded Academy of Light can finally make a proper effort at bringing through the next generation of Sunderland players, with facilities that are the envy of many other top European clubs. That is Murray's legacy and it will serve the club and the people of the city well in future years.

Getting it right on the field is a task that needs to be carried out immediately, and careful player recruitment is the only way it can be done. To achieve it, Roy Keane has needed money and plenty of it. Fans began salivating months before promotion was achieved when Niall Quinn spoke of an eight-figure sum being available to Keane in the summer of 2007, regardless of whether the club went up or not, and supporters' expectations were over-inflated accordingly.

Within minutes of the season's end the message boards of supporters' websites were littered with rumours and supposed sightings of world-class players who were falling over themselves to get to the Stadium of Light and climb aboard the magic carpet ride. If some of these rumours were to be believed, Ruud Van Nistelrooy was poised to turn his back on his luxurious Madrid lifestyle and set up home somewhere in the north east of England. Meanwhile, there were so many confirmed sightings of Paul Scholes in north east hotels and taxis throughout June and July that it was perfectly feasible that the ginger midfield schemer was employing a look-alike solely for the purpose of winding up Sunderland football fans.

For a lark, the club's official website safc.com decided to keep a record of all the players who Sunderland had been linked with in the press over the summer. By July 31st, the site's 'Rumour Mill' had 61 names on it, ranging from players as decorated as Scholes, Neil Lennon, Nicky Butt and Robbie Fowler to up-and-coming youngsters like Feyenoord's Royston Drenthe and Liverpool's Scott Carson. There were a few utterly unhinged entries too, former Newcastle United layabout Laurent Robert being the most notable.

When the wheeling and dealing did finally get underway, to many, the quality of recruits was underwhelming. First in was Greg Halford, a player who had joined Reading six months earlier but couldn't actually get into their team. He was followed by Russell Anderson, an Aberdeen centre-half who couldn't actually get into the Scotland team. This wasn't what was expected – fans wanted high-cash swoops for household names, signings that would get them talking in the street and raving in the pubs and clubs.

Keane's next signing finally got them talking – Cardiff City's Michael Chopra, signed for £5 million, and a section of the supporters were apoplectic. Five million for a player who'd scored 22 goals in the Championship last season? A bit on the expensive side but it was nine goals more than David Connolly got for Sunderland, so what was the problem? Well, Chopra was a Newcastle boy – he was brought through the ranks at St James' and scored for fun at every level, but chose to leave and seek glory elsewhere when he found his path to the first team was being continually blocked.

For Sunderland fans, Chopra was the enemy; there was no way he could play for Sunderland and give 100% week in and week out. They hadn't forgotten the goal he scored in the Magpies' 4-1 win at the Stadium of Light in 2006, or the way he taunted them after scoring two goals for Cardiff on Wearside later that same year. To be fair, the lad did endure 90 minutes of good, solid vitriol from the home faithful that night, so he could hardly be blamed for crowing a bit when he scored.

For too many Mackems, it was Lee Clark all over again. Clark played out of his skin for Sunderland for two years, but was then stupid enough to wear a T-shirt mocking the people who were paying his wages. He later said he could never have played against his beloved

Toon in the red and white of Sunderland. A similar lack of commitment is expected from Chopra by many, but the signing could turn out to be a masterstroke by Keane. He'll be reminding the player that he's got more to prove to the fans than any of the other summer signings – with a bit of luck, Chopra will raise his game that bit further and get the 15 goals that Sunderland will need from a striker if they are to prosper in the top flight. One rumour that Chopra had a Newcastle United badge tattooed on his arm and wouldn't be allowed to sign for Sunderland until he had had it laser-removed could neither be confirmed nor denied.

Chopra was also seen by many as a second choice signing after Keane had pulled out of a deal with Preston North End for their striker David Nugent. A fee of around £6 million had been agreed between the clubs while Nugent was away with the England under-21 squad, taking part in the European Championships. Upon returning, Sunderland and the player discussed terms and Nugent went off on holiday to think it over – a whole week later and he still hadn't made up his mind. Around about the same time that Nugent was airborne and heading back to England, Keane contacted Preston and told them the deal was dead.

Keane's reasoning will have been that if it takes Nugent an entire week to make up his mind then he doesn't want to sign for the club badly enough. Therefore he is not going to be allowed to become a Sunderland player. End of story. Nugent was believed to be holding out for a switch to his boyhood heroes, Everton, a move which in the end didn't materialise. Instead, he was sentenced to a four-year contract with Portsmouth. Nugent later protested that he'd needed time to consider the move fully and that Keane had been impatient in abandoning the deal when he did.

The Sunderland boss was unwavering, saying, 'I wasn't impatient with Nugent. I waited five weeks. If he thinks that is me being impatient he doesn't know me.'

More big money was splashed out on Manchester United's Kieran Richardson. Despite being an established England international, Richardson had never truly established himself at Old Trafford and most of his rave reviews came from a loan spell at West Bromwich Albion in 2005–06, when his performances were a major part of the Baggies' successful battle against relegation. Played mostly out of position at left-back upon his return to Old Trafford, the jury was still out on Richardson as he signed for Sunderland for £5.5 million in July but he'd certainly get more first team action with the Black Cats than he would have if he'd stayed in Manchester.

The David Nugent saga looked like repeating itself when Sunderland agreed a fee with Wigan Athletic for their left-back Leighton Baines. As with the Preston striker, the player held talks with Roy Keane and a deal looked likely until Baines 'pulled a Nugent' and opted out, also waiting for his boyhood club, also Everton, to come in for him, which in his case they eventually did.

Why a player would choose to play at run-down old Goodison instead of in front of 48,000 fans at the Stadium of Light is bewildering. Maybe it's the free toffee they throw around.

The Championship was raided for two more signings in July 2007 – centre half Paul McShane (£2.5 million) from West Bromwich Albion and central midfielder Dickson Etuhu (£1.5 million) of Norwich. Both are strong, aggressive, no-nonsense types of players, who should fit into Keane's team plan and thrive in the top flight. Keane knows all about McShane as the player was a trainee at Manchester United before signing for West Brom, and the defender shone during Sunderland's 2007–08 pre-season, looking to have secured himself a regular first team place before a ball is kicked in the Premier League.

Four days before the season kicked off, Sunderland smashed their record transfer fee as well as the British record fee for a goalkeeper for Hearts' Craig Gordon, paying £9 million pounds for the player who was rated by many as the best young 'keeper in Britain. Gordon signed despite major interest from Martin O'Neill at Aston Villa and the deal sent out the message that Keane and Quinn were definitely not in this for half-measures or mere survival. Perhaps Keane followed the advice of his first early mentor Brian Clough who built his league and European Cup-winning team around the signing of Peter Shilton, telling anyone who'd listen that having the best goalkeeper in the country would be worth 15 points over the course of the season. Gordon may not have been the best in the summer of 2007, but his recruitment, along with that of former Manchester United stopper Raimond Van Der Gouw as Sunderland's new goalkeeping coach, proved that Sunderland meant business.

Sunderland had never before made such an impression in the transfer market as they did in 2007. The £10 million double signing of Tore Andre Flo and Marcus Stewart in 2002 doesn't count – that was a crazed, desperate deal, made hours before the transfer window closed, akin to a man getting a leopard-skin scarf for his wife five minutes before the shops shut on Christmas Eve because he's forgotten to buy her anything else.

Splashing the cash to try and ensure Premier League survival was imperative in 2007. It was the year when the new, improved TV rights deal came into play, where the team who finished bottom of the league would still be rewarded with at least £30 million. What was a gap between the haves and the have nots in the world of English football was about to become a gulf.

The timing of Drumaville's intervention into Sunderland's affairs had to happen when it did. A year later and the club could have been consigned to the backwaters of the lower leagues indefinitely. With Niall Quinn at the helm, the supporters can finally be comfortable that their club has a custodian who they can trust implicitly.

Quinn knows the heights that the club can reach when results are going their way. He knows all about the passion and intensity which the fans feel for the club – as he memorably once said himself, 'I learned my trade at Arsenal, became a footballer at Man City, but Sunderland got under my skin. It hurt me deeply to leave. I love Sunderland.'

To hear Quinn describe Drumaville's motivation as a sporting challenge was refreshing in this day and age, where the Premier League is fast becoming a haven for foreign owners buying up clubs and saddling them with oceans of debt, chasing a quick profit that they won't necessarily get. Sunderland fans should feel far more comfortable about the future of their club than their counterparts at West Ham or Manchester City.

While the majority of profit-hungry clubs are currently chasing dollars in the Asian market in as many different ways as they can dream up, Drumaville are content for now to keep it closer to home and strengthen their Irish ties. Thanks to the Keane and Quinn connection, Sunderland are becoming the second (or sometimes first) team for more and more football fans just across the Irish Sea.

The team's pre-season friendly tour of the Irish Republic in late July was an enormous success and it would be no surprise to see it become an annual event.

Additionally, demand was outstripping supply for seats on flights from Ireland that coincided with Sunderland's home games last season, and it looks set to become a ritual for a new breed of Irish Mackems.

As the beginning of the season approached and with half a new team signed, it would be fair to say that the Premier League holds no fear for Roy Keane – after all, he's been there, done that and won the medals more than a few times with Manchester United.

Like Peter Reid before him, Roy Keane has a stubborn streak and is to be crossed at one's peril, but unlike Reid, he hasn't aligned himself to one style of play from which he'll struggle to deviate whenever circumstances demand it.

Keane shares Reid's fondness for the team ethic to override everything else, and looks at a player's character as much as anything else – the Irishman also has a near-pathological obsession with self-improvement and seeks the same in his players. Although he has just one managerial achievement to his name, Keane is potentially a great manager and could possibly even go on to be among the very best – that'll certainly be his aim, though he'd never admit to it.

Thanks to Keane and Niall Quinn, August 2007 would be the first time in six years, when Sunderland fans could look forward to a season in the Premier League knowing that they will see their team compete instead of capitulate.

Following the 2007 FA Cup semi-final between Chelsea and Blackburn which he attended, the Sunderland manager said of the two teams, 'What did I make of them? I think we would have taken either of them. Seriously? On the weekend's performance, I think we would.'

You never know, he might just be right.

Sunderland AFC 2006–07

Aug 6	Coventry City	L	1-2	A	22,366	Murphy
Aug 9	Birmingham City	L	0-1	H	26,668	
Aug 12	Plymouth Argyle	L	2-3	H	24,377	Murphy, S Elliott
Aug 19	Southend United	L	1-3	A	9,848	Stead
Aug 28	WBA	W	2-0	H	24,242	Whitehead, Neill Collins
Sep 9	Derby County	W	2-1	A	26,502	Brown, Wallace
Sep 13	Leeds United	W	3-0	A	23,037	Miller, Kavanagh, S Elliott
Sep 16	Leicester City	D	1-1	H	35,104	Hysen
Sep 23	Ipswich Town	L	1-3	A	23,311	De Vos (og)
Sep 30	Sheffield Wed	W	1-0	H	36,764	Leadbitter
Oct 14	Preston NE	L	1-4	A	19,603	Varga
Oct 17	Stoke City	L	1-2	A	14,482	Yorke
Oct 21	Barnsley	W	2-0	H	27,918	Whitehead, Brown
Oct 28	Hull City	W	1-0	A	25,512	Wallace
Oct 31	Cardiff City	L	1-2	H	26,528	Brown
Nov 4	Norwich City	L	0-1	A	24,852	
Nov 11	Southampton	D	1-1	H	25,667	Wallace
Nov 18	Colchester Utd	W	3-1	H	25,197	S Elliott 2, Connolly
Nov 24	Wolves	D	1-1	A	27,203	S Elliott
Nov 28	QPR	W	2-1	A	13,108	Murphy, Leadbitter
Dec 2	Norwich City	W	1-0	H	27,934	Murphy
Dec 9	Luton Town	W	2-1	H	30,445	Murphy, Connolly
Dec 16	Burnley	D	2-2	A	14,798	Leadbitter, Connolly
Dec 22	Crystal Palace	L	0-1	A	17,439	
Dec 26	Leeds Utd	W	2-0	H	40,116	Connolly, Leadbitter
Dec 30	Preston NE	L	0-1	H	30,460	
Jan 1	Leicester City	W	2-0	A	21,975	Hysén, Connolly
Jan 13	Ipswich Town	W	1-0	H	27,604	Connolly
Jan 20	Sheffield Wed	W	4-2	A	29,103	Yorke, Hysén, Connolly, Edwards
Jan 30	Crystal Palace	D	0-0	H	26,958	
Feb 3	Coventry City	W	2-0	H	33,591	Yorke, Edwards
Feb 10	Plymouth Argyle	W	2-0	A	15,247	Connolly, Stokes
Feb 17	Southend Utd	W	4-0	H	33,376	Connolly, Hysen, John 2
Feb 20	Birmingham City	D	1-1	A	20,941	Edwards
Feb 24	Derby County	W	2-1	H	36,049	Connolly, Miller
Mar 3	WBA	W	2-1	A	23,252	Yorke, John
Mar 10	Barnsley	W	2-0	A	18,207	Leadbitter, Connolly
Mar 13	Stoke City	D	2-2	H	31,358	Whitehead, Murphy
Mar 17	Hull City	W	2-0	H	38,400	Evans, John
Mar 31	Cardiff City	W	1-0	A	19,353	Wallace
Apr 7	Wolves	W	2-1	H	40,748	Murphy, Wallace
Apr 9	Southampton	W	2-1	A	25,766	Edwards, Leadbitter
Apr 14	QPR	W	2-1	H	39,206	Whitehead, Leadbitter
Apr 21	Colchester Utd	L	1-3	A	6,042	Yorke
Apr 27	Burnley	W	3-2	H	44,448	Murphy, Connolly, Edwards
May 6	Luton Town	W	5-0	A	10,260	Murphy 2, Stokes, Wallace, Connolly

Best win: 5 - 0 (May 6 v Luton Town (A))
Heaviest defeat: 1 - 4 (Oct 14 v Preston North End (A))
Longest unbeaten run (league games): 17 (Jan 1 - Apr 14)
Longest losing run (league games): 4 (Aug 6 - Aug 28)

Attendance
Highest: 44,448 (Apr 27 v Burnley)
Lowest: 24,242 (Aug 29 v West Brom)
Average Home (League): 31,880

Leading goalscorers: Connolly - (13)
Most appearances: Whitehead - (44)

Transfer deals

In

Date	Player	Previous Club	Cost
July 19	Kenny Cunningham	Birmingham	Free
Aug 4	Darren Ward	Norwich	Free
Aug 8	Clive Clarke	West Ham	£400,000
Aug 11	Arnau	Barcelona B	Free
Aug 22	William Mocquet	Le Havre	Undisclosed
Aug 23	Tobias Hysén	Djurgårdens IF	£1.7m
Aug 31	Dwight Yorke	Sydney FC	£200,000
Aug 31	Graham Kavanagh	Wigan	£500,000
Aug 31	Stanislav Varga	Celtic FC	£800,000
Aug 31	Ross Wallace	Celtic FC	£300,000
Aug 31	Liam Miller	Manchester Utd	Free
Aug 31	David Connolly	Wigan	£1.4m
Oct 19	Lewin Nyatanga	Derby	Loan
Jan 2	Marton Fulop	Tottenham	£500,000
Jan 2	Jonny Evans	Manchester Utd	Loan
Jan 2	Carlos Edwards	Luton Town	£1.4m
Jan 8	Anthony Stokes	Arsenal	£2.0m
Jan 25	Danny Simpson	Manchester Utd	Loan
Jan 29	Stern John	Coventry	£200,000

Out

Date	Player	New Club	Cost
July 21	Kelvin Davis	Southampton	£1.0m
July 26	Julio Arca	Middlesbrough	£1.75m
July 31	Christian Bassila	Larisa (Greece)	Free
Aug 8	George McCartney	West Ham	£600,000
Aug 18	Dan Smith	Aberdeen	Undisclosed
Aug 25	Kevin Kyle	Coventry City	£600,000
Oct 13	Jonathan Stead	Derby	Loan
Oct 17	Andy Welsh	Leicester	Loan
Oct 23	Clive Clarke	Coventry	Loan
Nov 3	Kevin Smith	Wrexham	Loan
Nov 14	Tommy Miller	Preston	Loan
Nov 23	William Mocquet	Rochdale	Loan
Nov 23	Arnau	Southend	Loan

Jan 2	Liam Lawrence	Stoke	£500,000
			(rising to a possible £650,000)
Jan 2	Robbie Elliott	Leeds Utd	Free
Jan 2	Ben Alnwick	Tottenham Hotspur	£900,000
			(rising to a possible £1.3m)
Jan 5	Neill Collins	Wolves	£125,000
Jan 8	Rory Delap	Stoke	Free
Jan 9	Kevin Smith	Dundee	Loan
Jan 11	Jonathan Stead	Sheffield Utd	£750,000
			(rising to a possible £1.25m)
Jan 11	Chris Brown	Norwich City	£325,000
Jan 31	Steven Caldwell	Burnley	£400,000